LESS STRESS,
MORE PEACE

Also by Verna Birkey

You Are Very Special
If God Is in Control, Why Is My World Falling Apart?
God's Pattern for Enriched Living
You: A People Helper

LESS STRESS, MORE PEACE

FINDING CONTENTMENT IN A HECTIC WORLD

VERNA BIRKEY

Fleming H. Revell

A Division of Baker Book House Co
Grand Rapids, Michigan 49516

© 1986, 1995 by Verna Birkey

Published by Fleming H. Revell
a division of Baker Book House Company
P.O. Box 6287, Grand Rapids, MI 49516-6287

Previously published as *God's Pattern for Contentment and Peace*

Printed in the United States of America

Library of Congress Cataloging-in-Publication Data

Birkey, Verna.
    Less stress, more peace : finding contentment in a hectic world / Verna Birkey.
        p.   cm.
    Includes bibliographical references.
    ISBN 0-8007-5555-3
    1. Spiritual life—Christianity. 2. Peace of mind—Religious aspects—Christianity. 3. Stress (Psychology)—Religious aspects—Christianity. I. Title.
    BV4501.2B523   1995
    248.4—dc20   94-39809

Unless otherwise noted, Scripture quotations are from the New King James Version. Copyright © 1979, 1980, 1982, Thomas Nelson, Inc., Publishers.

Scripture quotations marked NASB are from the New American Standard Bible, © the Lockman Foundation 1960, 1962, 1963, 1968, 1971, 1972, 1973, 1975, 1977.

Scripture quotations marked NIV are taken from the HOLY BIBLE, NEW INTERNATIONAL VERSION ®. NIV ®. Copyright © 1973, 1978, 1984 by International Bible Society. Used by permission of Zondervan Publishing House. All rights reserved.

Scripture quotations identified Phillips are from The New Testament in Modern English, Revised Edition, J. B. Phillips, translator, © J. B. Phillips, 1958, 1960, 1972. Used by permission of Macmillan Publishing Co., Inc.

CONTENTS

How to Get the Most from This Book

Stress! Stress! Stress! The word surrounds us in radio interviews, in books and magazines, on the lips of our coworkers, in the unspoken frustration of a harried young mother, in the unfulfilled longings of a lonely single. We feel it in our own fast-paced lives and sometimes in the testy responses of family and friends.

Even though, inevitably, we must be a part of this stress-filled world—a world of change, uncertainty, disappointment, confusion, rejection, and misunderstanding—there is a way to experience contentment and peace. This book is based on the confident assurance that there is a God-given way of relieving, managing, and rising above the daily stresses of life.

The apostle Paul knew that way. He declared, "I have learned in whatsoever state I am, to be content" (Phil. 4:11). He was satisfied to the point where he was not disturbed or disquieted no matter what happened to him. He had learned, in any and every circumstance, the secret of facing every situation. (See Phil. 4:11 in the

7

Amplified Bible.) What God did for Paul is gloriously available to every child of God.

The purpose of this book is to unfold, like the petals of a flower, the secret of facing every situation and coming out the winner. The prize is contentment and peace. You will find *Less Stress, More Peace* a helpful guide to your personal study. Answering the questions in the study guide will challenge you to think through the concepts in the book. You may want to record your responses in a journal or notebook.

This book may also be used in one-on-one discipling. Read the book together with someone you are encouraging and/or discipling. Work the exercises alone and come together for discussion and sharing. Husbands and wives will also enjoy working through it together.

In group study with your family, a group of friends, a Bible study group, or a Sunday school class *Less Stress, More Peace* is an interesting study. Members of the group can read a section and answer the questions on their own and then come together for discussion.

As the chapters unfold, my prayer is that you will experience the peace of God in every circumstance and be able to minister that peace to others.

ACKNOWLEDGMENTS

I am deeply indebted:

To Jeanette Turnquist, my longtime friend and teammate in ministry, for her tireless and patient rewriting and editing. To her also, gratitude for the study guide, and for the design of the diagrams throughout.

To Larry Crabb for the inspiration of his godly teaching, especially the concept of Personal Circle, which we have adapted to this teaching on contentment and peace.

To the women of the Enriched Living Workshops for their continued encouragement and enthusiastic support and for sharing so freely out of their lives.

To the saints of all generations who knew the secret of peace in every circumstance and who shared it with me in their wonderful books—the apostle Paul, F. B. Meyer, Andrew Murray, Oswald Chambers, Amy Carmichael, J. Sidlow Baxter, and countless more.

And, most of all, to my Lord, Jesus Christ, who fills that "last aching abyss" of my being with his peace.

PART 1

GOD'S HANDLE
FOR STRESS

1

STRESS: WHAT IS IT?

I received a desperate phone call one day from a dear young woman who was under tremendous stress. Six months earlier she had returned to the United States from Japan with her two small children. Her husband, still in Japan, had six more months before he fulfilled his assignment there.

During the past six months she hadn't heard a word from him. The last thing he had said to her before she left Japan was, "I really don't know if I want to continue this marriage. I'll let you know when I see you next year."

Her confused and desperate question to me was, "What shall I do? Should I give up on him and assume he doesn't want me? Should I try to find someone else? I thought I had been coping well. I enjoy my work. My children have a good baby-sitter, but my doctor said I'm suffering from depression. He said I need to deal with my stress. What do you think I should do?"

Of all the many ways in which the mind can cause the body to become ill, the most common is through the way we handle stress. As surely as dark clouds produce rain, prolonged stress will produce illness if it is not managed correctly. Situations causing stress take many different forms.

In one case, a mother ached for a daughter. I had a note from this mother, who had three sons whom she loved very much.

So why, Verna, do I still long for a daughter? Why do I still get a gnawing in my heart when I see a mother and daughter? Or when I meet an old school friend and she says, "Didn't have a girl, huh?" And I feel so sad when our church's mother-daughter banquet comes each year.

Why can't I accept the Lord's will more graciously? I hate myself at times for not letting go. In my mind I have given myself totally to God, but my heart must still be going its own way. How can I find relief from this desire?

In another case, a wife and mother battled cancer. Recently, I went to the funeral of a dear friend who had been battling cancer. For eight years she had been courageous, positive, and full of faith. How had she coped with the pain, the uncertainty of the future, the possibility of leaving a husband and four growing children when it seemed they needed her so much? What was her secret?

How could her husband cope with his loneliness and grief and the new responsibility of raising four children without her? Where is the victory for him?

In teaching women's workshops from Seattle to Omaha to Lancaster, from Uganda to Northern Ireland, and countless spots in between, I'm continually asked questions like, How do I cope with

three preschoolers who are demanding my attention
all day?
a pregnant daughter; a homosexual son?
singleness, especially when I'm so lonely and feel so
unwanted?
a husband who's chemically dependent?
the empty nest after my life has revolved around my
children for twenty-five years?
living with a husband who disciplines in anger and
has lost the respect of the children?
sick, elderly parents who must live with us now?
a loved one involved in pornography?
the demanding, tiring, and frustrating life of a single
working mother?
my husband's desire that I watch dirty movies with
him?
put-downs from some friends because I have no need
or desire to work outside the home?
making a career change; or entering the workforce
as a widow when I haven't worked outside my
home for thirty years?
financial distress and my husband's blame for letting
him make a bad investment?

Each of these situations is a legitimate, stressful circumstance. In each case things are not going the way
they were planned, expected, or hoped. Each person
must make a choice as to how she is going to respond
to the stressful circumstances. By not properly managing our stress we add more stress to the already difficult
situation.

What Is Stress?

By definition, stress is the response of the body to the
pressures and demands put on it. This physical response

may be activated by external or internal pressures such as changes in life's events or changes in our attitudes or beliefs.

Stress is not always negative or harmful. It can be a helpful motivator, a stimulant to greater achievement, or a mobilizer of the body's defenses to meet life's emergencies. Positive stress can result in increased energy, alertness, and enthusiasm. It can be an antidote to boredom and dullness.

Negative stress or stress overload can be harmful, especially if experienced over a prolonged period of time. This harmful stress can cause bodily illness or depression. It often comes when we resent or have a negative attitude toward unfavorable circumstances that we cannot control.

We need to learn how to manage stress so we can diminish the harmful effects and let it work for us in a positive and beneficial way.

2

GOD'S HANDLE FOR STRESS

She was a sixty-five-year-old woman with a bitter spirit. Four months earlier her forty-one-year-old daughter had died. Now Grandma's resentful attitude was not only making her own life miserable but was also adding to the heavy sorrow of her son-in-law and grandchildren. A neighbor commented, "She was such an active churchgoer all her life, but now it doesn't look as though her religion did her any good. She is just making life miserable for herself and others around her." This woman chose to believe that she could be happy only if her daughter were still around to help her and be her friend.

How does the person in a stressful situation deal with the resentment that tends to spring up when she has no way to control or change her difficult circumstances?

Jesus promised, "I have come that they may have life, and that they may have it more abundantly" (John 10:10).

Where does the abundant life that Jesus promised fit into the picture? Is there a handle for stress that actually works? Is it possible to experience a peace that passes all understanding (Phil. 4:7)? Can God's peace

> lower our blood pressure?
> lessen our stomach acid?
> calm our ulcers?
> release us from tension headaches?
> lessen our agitation and anxiety?
> make life not only bearable but victorious?

The real people of the Bible faced many and varied stressful situations such as most of us will never face.

Take, for example, Joseph (Gen. 37–50). Joseph experienced great pressure and strain as a result of his being hated, mistreated, and sold as a slave by his brothers. For two years Joseph was forgotten by the butler and left in a stinking Egyptian prison (Gen. 40:23). Yet Joseph's attitude seemed to be, "It's all right, Lord. I believe in your goodness. Your plan for my life is only good. You are adequate for me, even if I am hated and mistreated by my own brothers and forgotten by the butler." He was surrounded by stressful situations and stress-producing relationships. But his declaration of faith in God was simple, "You [brothers] meant evil against me, but God meant it for good" (Gen. 50:20 NASB).

Jonah (Jonah 1–4) is another good example of a person who faced stress. Jonah's whole experience of running from God's will was full of stress. Could you be swallowed by a great fish and not feel a little tension? But Jonah prayed from the depth of the fish's belly, "I called out of my distress to the LORD, and He answered me . . . While I was fainting away, I remembered the LORD: and my prayer came to Thee . . . Salvation is from the LORD" (Jonah 2:2, 7, 9 NASB).

Jonah knew how to grab the handle that could give him God's method of stress management.

David (1 Sam. 17–19) also faced stress. Did David find God to be adequate as he protected his sheep from the lion and the bear, faced Goliath, and coped with Saul's hatred and violence? David's simple statement of faith in his loving, caring, and powerful God is probably the most well-known verse in all of Scripture, "The LORD is my shepherd; I shall not want" (Ps. 23:1).

The apostle Paul (2 Cor. 11:23–28; 12:9–10) faced stress in ways that most people will never know. Paul was beaten, stoned, jailed, shipwrecked, and even left for dead. He had great physical weakness. One stressful event piled on top of another resulting in continual tension and strain. How did he handle it? Again and again Paul declared his faith in the living God. He rested in God's promise to him, "My grace is sufficient for you" (2 Cor. 12:9).

These great men took God's handle for managing stress and experienced freedom, contentment, and peace in the midst of the most difficult, trying times. They recognized the good things that God accomplished through their experiences.

Many of us know the words that these giants of faith spoke to declare their faith. We have mottos of them hanging on our walls. We easily say, "The Lord is my shepherd, I shall not want." We may even be able to quote 2 Corinthians 12:9. But do we experience the peace of God, as they did, so that life becomes not only bearable but triumphant?

To help us begin to grasp God's handle for stress, which can lead us into this peace, we will look at the steps toward less stress and more peace in the next few chapters.

3

UNDERSTAND
HOW GOD MADE US

We are all born with deep, legitimate, God-given longings. The Scripture describes these longings as hunger and thirst.

Everyone who thirsts (Isa. 55:1).

My soul thirsts. . . ; My flesh longs (Ps. 63:1).

My soul longs (Ps. 84:2).

The longing soul, . . . the hungry soul (Ps. 107:9).

As the deer pants. . . , so pants my soul. . . . My soul thirsts (Ps. 42:1–2 NIV).

This longing is a strong drive at the very core of our being. It's an inward demand, a feeling that must be satisfied at all costs. Let's call this drive, this demand, your

Figure 3.1

personal circle (see figure 3.1) and let it represent that deepest part of you that has

- longings
- thirsts
- desires
- needs

that are craving to be satisfied. Your personal circle is that part of you that has deep longings and reaches out to try to satisfy them in any way you think will quench the soul thirst that is always there. We tend to reach out to people or status or possessions to try to fill this longing, all the while not heeding what God says, "Ho! Everyone who thirsts . . . come to Me" (Isa. 55:1, 3).

The psalmist realized that ultimately only God could satisfy the longings and thirsts of his personal circle.

O God, You are my God; . . . My soul thirsts for You; My flesh longs for You (Ps. 63:1).

My soul longs. . . , My heart and my flesh cry out for the living God (Ps. 84:2).

He satisfies the longing soul, And fills the hungry soul with goodness (Ps. 107:9).

As the deer pants. . . , So my soul pants for You, O God. My soul thirsts for God, for the living God (Ps. 42:1–2).

Each of us has this personal circle with its deep longings and intense drives. Think for a moment. What is the deep yearning of your heart? I too have a deep longing, a desire, yes, a demand within me.

I want to

be wanted by someone.

be of value to someone.

be accepted by someone just for who I am, not for how I perform.

be specially chosen by a significant person.

be loved unconditionally by this one who will be sensitive to and try to meet all my needs.

belong to someone, enjoying intimate fellowship, loving companionship, and oneness of heart and purpose.

have a two-way commitment with someone—the other person to me, I to the other.

have meaningful, worthwhile, challenging work we can do together.

The Perfect Husband

Friends, husband, mother, daughter, challenging work—all can help fill that deep empty spot of longing to a certain degree. But even the most devoted and caring husband cannot (or should not be expected to) meet the deepest longings of a wife's heart. One great error that couples make is to believe that when they marry, the other person is going to be delighted to spend the rest of his or her life meeting the beloved's needs.

Most of us easily relate to Gloria's story.

Last night I thought Danny and I would have the evening alone. We had been running here and there all week and I longed for some time together. Our neighbor came over during dinner and Danny, knowing some deep needs she has, invited her to have dinner with us. She stayed for two hours. When she left, Danny buried his head in the newspaper. My inward reaction was to groan, Danny, can't you see I wanted us to be alone tonight?

No, there is no perfect husband, but God. Isaiah 54:5 says, "For your Maker is your husband; The LORD of hosts is His name." How many of us can actually say that at any given moment we have found God to be this "perfect husband" to us, satisfying our all-consuming demands for someone who will

> meet all our needs?
> enjoy our companionship?
> affirm us as a person?
> never let us down?
> never disappoint us?
> never fail to know our needs?
> never fail to be there when we need him?
> work harmoniously with us?

Only God can perfectly fulfill these desires, these longings for such a perfect and supportive relationship.

4

IDENTIFY
OUR LONGINGS

That we all have deep longings for something is evident throughout Scripture. We have seen that they are legitimate, God-given longings (see figure 4.1). To describe these inward longings and demands more specifically we could say we each have a longing to know and to sense that we belong, that we are worthwhile, and that we are competent.

Belonging

We all need to know that we belong, that we are loved, cared for, and accepted fully by someone of significance to us. We need to be wanted and desired. We want to feel that we are a part of someone.

Tiffany had a strong desire to know she still belonged after her new baby sister came home from the hospital. Her mother wrote to me.

Figure 4.1

Tiffany sat down beside me and said, "Mommy, I wish you hadn't gone to the hospital." I held my breath, but God gave me the wisdom and grace to calmly ask, "Why do you say that?" So she said honestly, "Because I want to be the only child."

At that moment he gave me this illustration. "Tiffany, when God sent you to live with Mommy and Daddy, he sent a bucket of love with your name on it and placed it within our hearts. This bucket is so big it will never be empty. When God gave us our next present, he sent another bucket with her name on it. We won't have to take any of the love from your bucket for our new baby because she has her own." As I shared this, her spirit sighed with relief as she snuggled closer. She belonged. She was loved. She was wanted!

Worth

We need to know and to sense that we are of value, we're acceptable, we count. To have a proper sense of worth is to have a sense of being right and doing right. It is to feel good about yourself because you are accepted by others. We have this assurance when we sense other people's positive attitudes toward us and when we feel that they approve of our actions or accept us irrespective of our actions.

Some careless words overheard at a sensitive time in her life added fuel to a very low sense of self-esteem that affected every aspect of Allison's future life.

When I was sixteen I overheard my mother and sister talking. My sister made the comment, "Allison is so pretty." Mother's reply was, "Allison is not pretty, she's cute." Ever since then when I look in the mirror I think, I'm not pretty.

This has affected my relationship with my husband and with my friends. When they tell me I look nice, I automatically say, "Oh, you don't really mean it."

Whether or not Allison's mother meant those few quick words as a put-down is not the point. Allison took the words into her teenage, worth-starved soul and concluded, "Since I'm not pretty, I'm of no value, no good, not acceptable."

After a meeting in Florida, Libby handed me this powerful statement of her mother's love.

When I was seven, I did something for which my mother had to discipline me. Angry at having been disciplined, I took a ballpoint pen and wrote on my bed sheet, "I hate you!" The next day Mother didn't say anything to me about what I had done. That night while sleeping I kept hearing a piece of paper crackling by my ear. The next morning I discovered a note my mother had pinned to my sheet (over what I had written), "Libby, you may not love us, but we certainly love you."

This broke me and I ran to my mother in tears to tell her I was sorry and that I really did love her. She hugged and kissed me. Twenty years later this still reminds me that Mother looked beyond my "bad mouth" and was able to accept me for who I was. She communicated that acceptance in a powerful way.

Competence

We also need to have a feeling of adequacy, of courage, of confidence, of hopefulness, of strength to carry out the daily tasks of life. We need to know and to feel that we *can*. Marcia testified about her discovery of God's purpose for her life.

> *When you said we are uniquely made by God for a special purpose, it hit me in a new way today. God made me to be my husband's wife! What a comforting revelation! I have so often felt that I was inadequate to be the right kind of wife for my very special husband. I've even been tempted to wonder if he would have been happier if he had married someone else. I no longer feel that way. My goal is to be the best wife I can be, by God's grace. I now believe he will make me adequate—to be what I ought for my dear husband.*

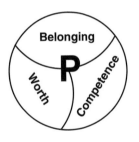

Figure 4.2

Add worth and competence to belonging, and you have a description of our triad of personal-circle needs. Each of us has a personal circle with these three longings crying out to be fed, to be satisfied, to be recognized as legitimate, God-given desires (see figure 4.2). From now on we will let this symbol represent our triad of personal needs.

As we try to understand this triad of needs, we must first know that a Christian has all the resources of the triune God to meet his or her triad of personal-circle needs.

5

God Is
Sufficient

As a redeemed child of God, I have the triune God to meet my triad of personal-circle longings—my personal needs, desires, and thirsts (see figure 5.1).

Our Need for Belonging

God the Father fundamentally meets our needs for belonging, for love, and for care. Our heavenly Father has received us and made it possible for us to belong to his family, through Christ. "As many as received Him, to them He gave the right to become children of God" (John 1:12). Now we can cry to him, "Abba Father" (Rom. 8:15). He is in control of the circumstances that touch us and will work them all together for good (Rom. 8:28). We did nothing to earn his love, but we are always wanted by

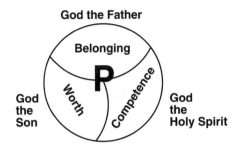

Figure 5.1

him and loved by him with an unconditional, voluntary love. We belong to his family.

> Yes, I have loved you with an everlasting love (Jer. 31:3).

> You were precious in My sight, . . . And I have loved you (Isa. 43:4).

> This one will say, "I am the LORD's," . . . And another will write on his hand, "Belonging to the LORD" (Isa. 44:5 NASB).

Our Need for Worth

God the Son fundamentally meets our needs for acceptance and worth. Guilt is a powerful force that destroys our sense of worth. A sense of guilt gives us the feeling that we are a nobody—a bad person, unacceptable, and insignificant. Jesus Christ died on the cross to pay the penalty for all our sins, to forgive our sins, to give us his righteousness, to free us from guilt, and to give us worth. Freedom from guilt opens the way for us to know and believe we are of value in God's eyes. Those he has redeemed, he wants to enlist and equip as his partners in ministry (see 2 Cor. 5:18–21). My value is determined by the price he paid: Jesus died for me! I am accepted in him.

> We have redemption through His [Christ's] blood, the forgiveness of sins (Col. 1:14).

> Through His [Christ's] name everyone who believes in Him receives forgiveness of sins (Acts 10:43 NASB).

Our Need for Competence

God the Holy Spirit gives us the competence, the power, and the ability to perform God's assignments and glorify him. He pours out the love of God in our hearts. He gives joy, peace, and longsuffering, enabling us to manifest the fruit of the Spirit, and he gives us strength to face our particular situations day by day (see Rom. 5:5; Rom. 8:26; Gal. 5:22–23).

> I am full of power by the Spirit of the LORD (Micah 3:8).

> God has not given us a spirit of fear, but of power and of love and of a sound mind (2 Tim. 1:7).

The triune God is enough to meet our deepest longings, to fill our personal circle. Each of us has a God-shaped vacuum that only God can fill. To know that I belong to him, that I'm part of his family, that he loves and cares for me, and that he promises to cause all things to work together for my good means more to me than the love, care, or belongingness that I sense through any human being, no matter how dear that person is to me. To know my sins are forgiven, my guilt is gone, and that I am fully accepted in Christ means more to me than acceptance from any person on earth. And to know that the Holy Spirit wants to equip me to do all the will of God, enabling me to make a significant impact for him on others around me, and that he gives me the inner power to be thankful, joyful, patient, and loving is more important than the strongest affirmation I could receive from another human being. The bottom line is that God is and always will be sufficient.

However, to meet our personal-circle longings it is God's plan for the human and the divine to work together. In addition to his love and acceptance, he plans that we sense and receive love and acceptance from other human beings. (In part 4 we take up in detail the human side of God's plan.) But when the human fails, we must still hold on to the fact that God himself—and what he chooses to provide at that moment—is ultimately enough to meet our needs. What he chooses to provide usually includes a generous supply of other good things too. It is the same as saying, "The LORD is my shepherd; I shall not want" (Ps. 23:1).

Can We Manage Our Reactions?

The amount of stress we experience is determined not so much by what happens to us but by our reaction to what happens to us. We have said that what God provides is enough to meet our needs. Too much stress comes more from our attitude toward God's provision than from the actual circumstances. Therefore, the basic question in getting a handle on stress is, "How can we properly manage or control our *reaction* to stressful or potentially stressful situations?"

As I was driving to church one Sunday I was thinking about personal-circle fullness. Because I travel so much, I'm at my own church very few Sundays each year and sometimes it's a scary thing for me to go to church. I wonder if there will be anyone around that I know, anyone that I can relate to. As I drove, I talked to the Lord, "Lord, I choose to believe that you, yourself, and what you decide to provide for me when I get to church will be all I need. Now Lord, I pray that there will be someone I can sit beside—someone who needs me. But if not, it's all right. Whether I sit alone or with someone, you—and the sense of your presence—are all I really need. I claim personal-circle fullness, full satisfaction, in you."

When I went in, I saw no one sitting alone. Everyone was busily engaged with family or friends. So I sat alone and no one even came close to me. The seats beside me were empty. The seats in front of me were empty. All I saw was emptiness.

My tendency before had been to think, *Oh, here I am alone again.* But not that morning! It didn't matter that there was emptiness around me. My personal circle was full! God had so filled me with the consciousness of his presence, his love, and his sufficiency that I felt like standing to sing the "Hallelujah Chorus" all by myself! I was not embarrassed. I was not lonely. It did not matter what people were thinking. I was free from myself so I could look around and pray for those around me.

What had made the difference? I had declared my faith by saying, "I choose to believe, Lord Jesus, that you yourself, and what you choose to provide at this moment, are all I need!" This brought me personal peace and victory in the midst of an otherwise stressful situation.

But as with all truth, we can so easily get off balance (see chapter 8). It is important that we aren't just passively content that God fills and satisfies our personal-circle longings (of belonging, worth, and competence) to the point that we cut ourselves off from others. We need each other. We are to be continually reaching out to others—giving love to them and receiving love from them.

The next Sunday as I drove to church the Lord and I talked again. He said, "My grace is sufficient for you again today, Verna." And I said, "Thank you, Father. I receive your grace. Now, Father, lead me to someone who is lonely. Someone who needs me."

Sure enough, there was a lady alone, someone I didn't know, and space enough for me to sit beside her. We greeted one another briefly and then after church spent twenty minutes sharing together. Yes, my own personal circle was full, but God had also chosen to provide human affirmation that day. What a thrill it was to affirm each other in our triad of personal-circle needs!

6

WHAT IS
OUR RESPONSIBILITY?

There was a very godly man who was convinced that he needed something changed in his life, that he needed something different from what he had. This man wanted to glorify God more than anything, and he was convinced that if this thing were changed he could do that better. He prayed and prayed and prayed again, earnestly asking the Lord to change his situation.

Yes, this man was Paul and he had a "thorn in the flesh" that he wanted removed (2 Cor. 12:7–10). Many interpret this as being eye trouble. Some say it was acute bodily pain and weakness that may have given him a repulsive appearance. Whatever that thorn was, it was something that touched Paul's personal-circle longings. It made him feel inadequate and weak, and he longed for it to be removed so he could feel strong and competent and perhaps be more acceptable in appearance.

Paul begged the Lord three times to remove the thorn. The Lord's answer was, "My grace is sufficient for you, for My strength is made perfect in weakness" (2 Cor. 12:9). God was saying, "My grace is all you need. You don't need this weakness removed. What you really need is my strength to replace your weakness. I am sufficient for your present need in this present condition. Trust me! I will supply what you really need to live adequately and joyfully in this present condition and to more perfectly fulfill my purposes for your life—that is, to glorify me. Trust me. Trust me!"

Paul's Choice Regarding His Thorn

Paul was faced with a decision. God was saying one thing; Paul felt another way. Was he going to choose to believe what God said? Or, was he going to choose to continue to believe that the thorn must be removed if he was to live life to the full?

God was saying, "It's not necessary to remove the thorn, Paul. That's not what you really need. I myself (my grace) and what I choose to provide for you at this moment are adequate for you."

What would you choose? To believe the words that God had spoken? Or to believe that the thorn must be removed?

Paul's choice is clear. "Most gladly, therefore, I will rather boast about my weaknesses, that the power of Christ may dwell in me. Therefore I am well content with weaknesses, . . . for Christ's sake; for when I am weak, then I am strong" (2 Cor. 12:9–10 NASB).

Paul chose to believe that God himself, and what he chose to provide for him at that moment, was all he needed. We could say that Paul's personal circle was full because he had come to the point where he was looking to God alone to satisfy the deepest longings of his being. He was not inwardly demanding something more or something different. Instead, he accepted God's way and took a positive attitude full of hope. Let me suggest that this is the way to the abundant life Jesus promised (John 10:10). This is the victory that overcomes the world (1 John 5:4). This is the way to manage our reactions to an undesirable and difficult situation and therefore to reduce our stress.

Choose
(in any given circumstance
    or situation)
to believe
that God himself,
and what he chooses to provide
at this moment,
is all I need
(at this moment).

Figure 6.1

At that moment of choice and faith our personal circle is full (see figure 6.1). We have peace and contentment.

What we choose to believe is very significant to our personal joy. Suppose Paul had chosen to believe that God's grace was not enough. Suppose he had chosen to continue believing that he did, indeed, need the thorn removed. If he had made such a choice, what would have happened to Paul on the inside? Would he have experienced contentment and peace? Or would he have been torn apart by frustration, inner conflict, and resentment?

My Worst Disappointment: Singleness

I received a letter from a forty-year-old woman who said she had been emotionally unstable for twenty years.

My worst disappointment is being single. I haven't even had any serious boyfriends. I grew up hearing in church that "My

God shall supply all your needs according to his riches in glory."
I am so disillusioned with God and Jesus. I don't believe he has
provided for my needs and I don't even know if I'm saved any-
more. Is God really alive?

What had she chosen to believe? That God himself
and what he would choose to provide for her were all
she needed? No, she chose to believe that she needed
marriage—at least boyfriends—to make her happy, to
meet her needs. She chose to believe that her personal-
circle longings would be satisfied *if* she had a husband.
God was not providing a husband at that moment so
she believed there was no way for her to have personal-
circle fullness.

Larry Crabb gives some excellent direction as to what
our responsibility is in experiencing personal-circle
fullness.

When I depend upon God's provision for my needs,
and not on what *I may think I need,* I will respond to
rejection not with anger but with deliberate thanksgiving in the midst of my sorrow. And it will be sin-
cere. So many at this point will say, "Be thankful for
so and so's rejection? Maybe I could bring myself to
say thank you, but I surely wouldn't mean it." But if
my mind is fixed on the staggering truth that the sov-
ereign God of the universe loves me and has pledged
Himself to provide me with everything I need, if I
really believe that, then I will sincerely (sometimes
with great difficulty but still sincerely) bow my knees
in thanksgiving when I experience the rejection of
another, not because God's love compensates for that
rejection but because God's love can work through
that rejection. . . . When the omnipotence and sovereignty of God are even feebly apprehended, I relax.
God will meet my needs. No one can stop His love or

the plans of His love. I am in His hands and there I rest secure.[1]

This thanksgiving Crabb speaks of is thanking God for these great truths about himself—his sovereignty, his loving care, and his promised faithfulness to me even in the midst of humanly desperate situations. This act of thanksgiving is an expression of my heart's surrender and confident trust that God will take even this rejection and cause it to be used for my good.

The "What-ifs" and "If-onlys"

A wife whose family was facing an uncertain future wrote to tell me how personal-circle fullness helped her to trust God.

> I have a bad case of the "if-onlys." My husband is now working half-time with half salary. The outflow has become greater than the income. Basically my attitude has been to trust, but there are times when I am tempted to panic, to worry, and I begin asking myself the "what-ifs" and the "if-onlys." How will we pay our bills? What if we get sick? What if he can't find a full-time job?
>
> The temptation to worry goes away when I direct my thoughts to God, knowing that
>
>> he loves me.
>> I belong to him.
>> he will provide for my family.
>> he will give me strength to accept whatever he has planned for me.
>> I will be able to handle any future situation because of his power.
>
> Knowing he is in control and I can trust him has caused me to choose to believe that God himself, and what he chooses

to provide at this moment, is all I need. My personal circle is full!

We have seen the first step in reducing our stress and moving toward a life of contentment and peace is to understand that God made us with deep, legitimate longings that ultimately he alone can satisfy. We really don't *need* anything more or different than what we have (though these things we want may be legitimate, enjoyable, and very affirming). God is ultimately enough to satisfy your triad of personal-circle longings. But you have a responsibility also. It's up to you to choose to believe that God himself, and what he is providing at this moment, is all you really need at this moment for personal contentment and satisfaction, for personal-circle fullness. You must declare your faith. You must reach out to apprehend the omnipotence, sovereignty, and love of God for your personal circumstances. One way you can do this is through making the following declaration of faith.

> My Declaration of Faith
> I choose to believe
> that God himself,
> and what he chooses to provide
> at this moment,
> is all I need.
> My personal circle is full.
> I am complete in Christ (Col. 2:10).

What God Chooses to Provide

Jeremy Taylor, a mighty preacher of the seventeenth century, even after his house was plundered, his family driven out, and his estate confiscated, could still write:

I am fallen into the hands of publicans and they have taken all from me. What now? They have not taken away my merry countenance, my cheerful spirit, and a good conscience; they have still left me the providence of God, and all His promises, my hopes of Heaven, and my charity to them, too. And still I sleep and digest, I eat and drink, I read and meditate. And he that hath so many causes of joy, and so great, is very much in love with sorrow and peevishness if he were to choose to sit down upon his little handful of thorns.[2]

What did Jeremy Taylor do with what God had chosen to provide (indicated by the marks in the personal circle in figure 6.2)? He chose not to sit on his handful of thorns, moaning and complaining about those things he wished he had but that God had chosen not to provide at that time. Rather, he chose to believe that God himself, and what he chose to provide at that moment, was all he needed. His personal circle was full!

Figure 6.2

7

CHOOSE TO BELIEVE

It is very important to realize that consciously or subconsciously, we are continually choosing to believe something—whether positive or negative. It is our belief system that so deeply affects our attitudes and behavior. If we are going to change our attitude or behavior, it is our responsibility to choose to believe the right thing. When I choose to believe that I *need* something more or different from what I have and the thing I desire is not happening, I can so easily get angry, irritated, or discouraged.

In the Psalms we read, "They believed His words; they sang His praise. . . . They did not believe His word, but murmured in their tents" (Ps. 106:12, 24, 25). If we believe and rest in God's sufficiency, we have peace. On the other hand, if we have an inward grumble or demand for something different, this blocks the flow of peace and the result is unrest, dissatisfaction, and discontent.

41

Like Paul, we must choose contentment by learning to take responsibility for our choices and realistically facing our inward demand for something more or something different.

A woman recently wrote to me that the joy had drained from her spirit.

My husband is a wonderful Christian husband and father. Our relationship is close and good. There is, however, one area that has caused me grief and anxiety. At times my husband's example of godly character before the children has been poor. He raises his voice, yells at the children, and responds to them with irritation. The kids respond back in the same way they are treated.

As I observe the reaction of the children to his poor responses, it has caused my joy to drain from my spirit as well as my face. My concern is that the children will not hear what we say if they do not see what we say. I know that godly truth cannot be imparted if negative example speaks louder.

I have approached Jim on several occasions in a poor manner, with poor results. I have also approached him in a proper and loving manner with the result that he recognizes the problem and wants to do right. But as time progresses, he regresses.

When I first heard the declaration of personal fullness, it really spoke to me in this situation. I made the choice to believe that in this situation God himself and what he chooses to provide at this moment are all I need.

I know that God is able to handle this situation and the outcome of godly character in my children. And he can do it even better without my anxious spirit. It truly is the will that must make this choice, because my emotions may take time to catch up.

Many times we do not realize that we can *choose* to believe. In fact, we are making that choice all day long.

Sometimes we choose to believe that God is being stingy and could really do better by us. But how different we feel and how much better the day goes when we consciously choose to believe that God himself, and what he chooses to provide at this moment, is all I need at this moment.

Another woman began her letter,

My husband gave up a good-paying job to become an executive in what seemed to be a growing, thriving company. He was now second man on the totem pole, working for an enterprising multimillionaire and drawing a very generous salary. We whipped around in his plush business car and enjoyed the many benefits of such a position.

After nine months of luxurious living, Ken began to see that things were not right. The company was in deep trouble—cash flow was low, credit was shot, salary checks bounced, promised benefits were withdrawn. Uncertainty has reigned now for two years, and the company has filed Chapter 11.

But I truly believe Ken and I are in God's place, at his time, and for his purpose. When he accomplishes all he wants to through these circumstances, he will change them! My personal circle is full! Even though it seems as if the roof is caving in and the bottom is dropping out, I have personal-circle fullness.

I don't know what I would have done during these long and difficult months if you hadn't shared with me about choosing personal-circle fullness. More than once during the day I look up to my Father with this declaration of faith: I choose to believe that God himself, and what he chooses to provide at this moment, is all I need. (In very difficult times I not only say "all I need," but "exactly what I need.") God has used this to bring me peace during an extremely stressful time.

This woman found that it is not so much the pressure or difficulty of our circumstance that causes us stress and anxiety as it is our inward response and our beliefs about ourselves and our circumstances. A good way to bring our hearts to the point of rest is to choose afresh to believe in God's promised sufficiency. We can make that choice and take that stand by repeating the declaration of faith statement—choosing to trust God and believe in his truth.

"Lord, a good Christian husband, please" is the prayer of this divorced woman.

I was divorced eight years ago and had an eighteen-month-old son to care for. For the past eight years I have so desired to be married again. I do all right on my own as a single parent, but sometimes the loneliness seems unbearable. I have prayed and cried and prayed some more for the Lord to bless my life with a good Christian husband.

In all eight years there has been no indication of my prayers being answered the way I want them. It has been so encouraging for me to see how happy and fulfilled you are, though single. I don't know if I will be single forever or if God will one day grant me a husband, but I feel a real peace about the personal-circle-fullness situation now. The Lord can fill my emptiness and will sustain me. Praise to him for his love!

A friend wrote,

I haven't yet had the privilege of attending your workshop on contentment and peace in a stressful world, but when you shared with me last week in Seattle a bit about personal-circle fullness, my heart confirmed what you were saying. Could I tell you one of my struggles that led me to finally claim and experience that completeness in Christ, that adequacy of God himself?

Many things have transpired to bring me to this place, not the least of which was an airplane trip I took with my family. I was terrified at the thought of flying.

I was so fearful and anxious that for the first time in my life I wondered if there even was a God. I desperately wanted a booming voice to say, "I'm here, don't give up," because if I couldn't believe in God anymore I had nothing. Since I heard no booming voice of reassurance (with an answering surge of confidence arising within), I realized it was all coming down to a choice: Would I believe God or wouldn't I? It seemed so cold and unspiritual and scary. Sort of like choosing my religion from the boxes of others on the store shelf.

I was just about at the place of choosing God and deciding I would take him at his word, with or without feelings, when I went to hear Elisabeth Elliot. Her message was so simple—trust and obey (just like you had said in Seattle). She gave several examples of when she had had to choose God when everything seemed absurd. It was essentially stuff I'd heard a thousand times before but it hit me as if I were hearing it for the first time. One of the things she said that jumped out at me was, "The most mature have suffered and endured." (Endurance hasn't been one of my strong points.) If I want to be mature, and I do, I have to trust God and forge ahead—not give up, not fall away, not murmur and complain. She also said, "The only thing we need to know is 'Trust God.'" All of that led me to choose to trust him, shakily but decidedly.

I was willing now to take that flight. I did jokingly say to my husband, "Why don't we drive?" When the wheels were stolen off our car that week it was as if God were jokingly saying to me, "See, you couldn't drive now if you wanted to." My neighbors couldn't understand why I thought having our wheels stolen was so funny.

At any rate, God did give me what I needed. First, he helped me see how foolish and futile it was to think the worst, imagining the plane crashing, my final moments, and my children dying with me. I began to discipline my mind. Second, the Power paper the day before we left was on fear and that helped. Third, I knew several people were praying for me. Fourth, I was reminded of the song, "Someday the Silver Cord Will Break," especially the line, "and I will see him face to face." At first it scared me. "Are you preparing me to die, Lord?" I asked. But it turned out to be my greatest comfort. On takeoffs I'd close my eyes and pray, "Will I get to see you today, Lord?"

It all boiled down to God and me. And it got me through. I had finally come to the place where I could declare, "I choose to believe that God himself, and what he chooses to provide, is all I need. My personal circle is full!" And it was.

Sometimes we choose to imagine the worst thing that could possibly happen to us. Our imagination produces fear, anxiety, and worry instead of peace. I recommend using this simple statement of faith as a vivid reminder of truth and an encouragement to make an on-the-spot choice to believe the truth.

8

BALANCING THE TRUTH

 God fills your personal circle. He and his present provision are all you need. Up to this point we have been basically talking about one aspect of this truth. We could call it the be-content end of the seesaw. There is another aspect of this same truth that we also must consider in order to keep the truth in balance. If we have tunnel vision for only one aspect of the truth, we will get that precious truth out of balance (see figure 8.1).

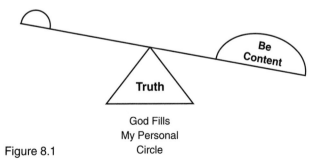

Figure 8.1

We need to continually realize the importance of walking toward the balance of truth. The human tendency is to walk away from balance into an extreme or perverted application of that truth.

The Danger of Passive Contentment

Even the blessed truth of personal contentment can have its dangers unless we balance it with the other side of this truth. As we learn more and more to find our longings met in God himself it's possible to become too passive. Instead of communicating with her husband and facing problems, a wife can use the lack of communication to escape the real world. For some it becomes so much easier to clam up and be a doormat.

The other side of this truth reminds me that God wants me to take responsibility to realize the will of God for me personally, for my family, and in all my relationships. That will no doubt include reaching out in love and care for others. It will mean actively fulfilling the responsibilities God gives. For example, a mother must be actively involved in raising her children to be obedient and respectful. As we add this other side of the truth (the importance of taking personal responsibility), the truth becomes balanced (see figure 8.2).

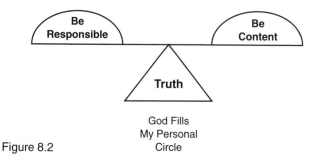

Figure 8.2

Several years ago on a plane trip across the country I was mistakenly assigned a seat in the smoking section. I knew that I would have some heavy responsibilities when I arrived on the East Coast, and after five hours in the smoking section, I would not be at my best. After checking with the agent at the gate, I found he was happy to hold my ticket until a nonsmoking seat might become available.

I had already chosen personal-circle fullness. Now if what God chose to provide that day included the smoking section, I would still be content. But in this case, I took responsibility to reach out in a right spirit and see if the will of God for me would include no smoke and thus make me more refreshed to be God's servant as I stepped off that plane. Being content and responsible balanced the truth for me that day.

Another example of balancing contentment with responsibility was my experience of going to church alone (see chapter 5). I learned that it's possible to rest in God as the only one who can ultimately meet my deep longings and at the same time actively reach out to befriend others and stretch myself to discover the will of God for me.

How do we know if a certain action is taking proper responsibility? It all hinges on motivation: Is this action my selfishly seeking to meet my own needs as an end in themselves? Or is this action a result of actively seeking the will of God, with a desire to submit to him whatever the outcome?

The Danger of Perverting the Truth

As I have illustrated, we are in danger when we weigh one side of the truth too heavily and don't balance it with another side of that truth. A second danger is to totally misunderstand the meaning of one side of the truth and pervert that aspect of the truth. A perversion is only a partial truth—a misunderstanding or misapplication.

Possible perversions for the "be responsible" side of the truth could be acting in a wrong spirit, acting apart from God, or reaching out selfishly to control my world to get something God is not now providing. Possible perversions for the "be content" side of the truth could be being too passive, not communicating, not facing the problem, or not reaching out to others. We might be sitting passively, being content, when there is an issue we need to address or a person we need to confront. One wife had a creative solution for confronting her husband about a need she felt.

Some time ago I had a problem getting my husband to spend time with me. He is a physician and often comes home late and really enjoys being alone. It seemed he never had time to listen to me or hear the concerns of raising our two sons.

One night as we were getting ready for bed I asked him how long he allotted his patients for an office visit. "Fifteen minutes," he said.

"And how much do you charge them?"

"Sixty dollars."

I went to the closet, took out my purse, and quietly and calmly handed him three twenty-dollar bills, asking for fifteen minutes of his undivided attention.

I talked, he listened. Then he advised, "You need to send your husband in. He really needs to listen to you more."

Now, months later, he not only asks me to share with him my concerns, but seems to know when I need to talk with him, and he suggests it first.

This dear one could have been passive when there was need to address a situation. For some personalities it may be far easier to sit back and say nothing, but they would miss God's best for them and not bring the most glory to his name.

J. Sidlow Baxter in his book *His Part and Ours* clarifies and enlarges on this balance between contentment and responsibility.

> Mind you, being content with our present circumstances does not mean that we are to be supinely unconcerned about present evils which we can help to remedy, but it does mean that we are to be content with that personal position in life which a beneficent, overruling Providence has seen proper for us; and it does mean also that we are to accept cheerfully those circumstances which are providentially permitted to surround us.
>
> Nor does being content with our present circumstances mean a sluggard indifference to self-improvement. Nay, if we are truly content with what God has seen good for us we will by grateful endeavor turn it to the best account. Let us remember, however, that true self-improvement does not mean merely a rise in our salary, a higher position, a larger house, a swell car, but a greater love to God, a clearer perception of His will and ways, a truer likeness to the character of Christ, a more generous love to our brother, a truer fulfilling of just that place and purpose in this present life which God has had in His heart for us to fill. This is the real, the true, the only ultimately worthwhile self-improvement.
>
> Contentment is to take joyfully all that comes to us from God's hand, and to acquiesce trustingly in the will of God when things are taken from us.[3]

We can take that position and come to that place of peace and contentment by again choosing our declaration of faith: "I choose to believe that God himself, and what he chooses to provide at this moment, is all I need."

9

STEPS TO REDUCE STRESS

It is not what happens to us, but our negative reaction to events that causes overstress in our lives. Because our reactions are very important, we have spent eight chapters discussing how to manage our inner attitude toward the external pressures we experience. By managing our attitude toward events we can, in partnership with God, take charge of our distress and let him transform it into a positive experience for good. The key is to deliberately hand over the situation to the Lord and trust him for the outcome, being confident and content in him, instead of being upset, angry, and resentful.

The way to handle stress is to declare in the midst of the trial: "I choose to believe that God himself, and what he chooses to provide at this moment, is all I need." This is a very realistic, down-to-earth way to actually surrender the situation to him, declare our trust in him, and rest in him for the outcome. In doing so, we experience the secret of being content in any and every situation and the peace that transcends all understanding that Paul talks about and that every committed child of God longs for (see Phil. 4:7, 11 NIV).

What Our God Is Like

I know with confident assurance that God loves me and cares for me affectionately and watchfully. He is interested in my best interests and in my personal well-being. He delights in giving me what is the very, very best for me. He is wide awake and in control of everything that touches me. He will not allow anything to come to me that is not included in the "all things" he promised to work together for my good (Rom. 8:28).

Therefore, by faith I choose to believe that he is presently working for my good. I hand all my concerns over to him. I trust him. That is, in the midst of each trial or pressure situation, instead of resenting it, I make this declaration of faith, "I choose to believe that God himself, and what he chooses to provide at this moment, is all I need." In this way I can be a partner with him to transform my

resentment into trustful acceptance.
demand for my own way into surrender to his will and way.
selfish, self-getting spirit into self-giving love.
doubting and questioning into trust.
critical, unforgiving spirit into forgiveness.
fear into faith.

Trusting God is the most crucial and basic thing you must do to diminish your stress. However, there are three other significant, practical things you must do if you want to reduce stress in your life.

Evaluate Your Lifestyle

Again and again in Psalm 42 the psalmist asked himself, "Why are you in despair, O my soul? And why have you become disturbed within me?" (Ps. 42:5, 11 NASB) It is as though he is saying to himself, What is it about your lifestyle that has brought you so low, made you so discouraged, so immobilized by circumstances? Evaluate your lifestyle as the psalmist did and, as Paul tells us, "have a sane estimate of your capabilities" (Rom. 12:3 PHILLIPS). If your lifestyle is causing stress overload, take the necessary steps to make the changes that will release you from your bondage to your own expectations and the demands of others.

> Are you trying to live beyond your limitations—physical, financial, and emotional? Learn to be content with who you are and what you have.
> Are your expectations, your goals, and your values totally impossible to live up to? Set realistic standards for yourself and rely on God's power to hold you up where your own strength lets you down.
> Are your attitudes weighted down with resentment, anger, anxiety? Refuse to carry this excess baggage.
> Are you being driven by someone else's agenda for your life? Let God's will dictate your plans.
> Are you living under time pressure? Delete, delegate, organize, and simplify your life.

The following rule can be applied to all the things that clutter and take the time out of your days: If it saves time, use it; if it doesn't work, fix it; if it can be eliminated, cancel it. This can be applied to anything from the newest kitchen gadget to that magazine you subscribed to that comes every month and makes you feel guilty because you don't have time to read it.

Let your personal limitations and abilities guide you in revising your lifestyle. Live realistically! On the other hand, expect to live supernaturally—discerning and following God's specific plan for you, trusting him to enable you to do that which is beyond your natural inclinations and gifts.

Are You a Driven Person?

Another important area in evaluating your lifestyle is to discern your motivation, that inner drive that causes you to do something or to act in a certain way. Ask and honestly answer, "Why am I doing what I'm doing?" Is it because

people expect me to do it?
I want to do it?
it brings personal enjoyment, caters to my pride, or gains acceptance and affirmation from others?
it's one of my spiritual gifts or special abilities?
I want to keep up with my peers?
I want to appear that I have it all together—spiritually, emotionally, and physically?
it fulfills me?

What are your reasons for doing what you're doing? That is, are you being driven by one or more of the above reasons? "Don't let the world around you squeeze you into its own mold, but let God remold your minds from within" (Rom. 12:2 PHILLIPS). Are you listening to the wrong voices, or are you listening to the voice of your Shepherd and following him? Jesus said, "My sheep hear my voice, . . . and they follow Me" (John 10:27).

Are you a following person? A following person senses God has a plan for him or her, a unique assignment from him, and that it is the very best. A following person is

Spirit-directed, Spirit-appointed, Spirit-gifted for the calling. A following person consults God and follows him in discerning and ordering her priorities for living.

Discern your motivation: Are you a driven person or a following person?

Honor Your Body

"Have you forgotten that your body is the temple of the Holy Spirit, who lives in you, . . . and that you are not the owner of your own body? You have been bought, and at what a price! Therefore bring glory to God in your body" (1 Cor. 6:19–20 PHILLIPS). Some of us have forgotten that as children of God we don't own our own bodies. We forget it when we overfeed them. We forget it when we neglect the body's basic needs.

My friend Connie Slay is a nurse who works with recovering cardiac patients. She gives stress seminars in which she emphasizes that there are three essential body-related needs to consider in minimizing stress: (1) exercise, (2) nutrition, and (3) rest and relaxation. Here are some interesting specifics from Connie.

Exercise

The Bible says that exercise "profits a little" (1 Tim. 4:8). And that is true compared to faith, but it does profit some. Exercise is one of the great stress reducers.

Under stress our bodies manufacture a chemical called adrenaline. It's there for our protection. If a bear takes after us, the adrenaline that our bodies quickly produce gives us power to climb a tree or fight him off. The blood clots quicker, the pupils dilate so that we can see better, our respiration goes up so we have more air, our heart rate goes up, our blood pressure goes up.

Blood is sent to the heart and the brain and away from organs that don't need it as much at that moment.

Our stress reaction is built into us for a reason. It is an automatic body-protection system. However, in the twentieth century, stress comes to us not necessarily in the form of bears, but in a variety of other ways throughout the whole day. And when it does, this same stress response happens to us to a greater or lesser degree. In fact, the definition of stress is a nonspecific response of our body to any demand upon it.

We can't necessarily run from trouble as we would from a bear—trouble at work, that person at home, that tough situation we face day after day that never goes away. But the hormones are still released to a greater or lesser degree. What we can do to combat stress, in addition to faith, is exercise.

Exercise uses up that adrenaline we would use up if we were running from a bear. It relaxes those muscles made tense and tight by stress. We run, walk, swim, bicycle, ski, or whatever else our choice might be. The benefits of exercise are numerous. It reduces blood pressure, heart rate, and cholesterol. It helps us sleep better, decreases depression and fatigue, and increases our self-image and endurance. Exercise not only helps reduce stress, it also helps prevent the devastating effects of stress.

Nutrition

It has been said that many of us, particularly in the United States, are digging our graves with our teeth. Six of the ten leading causes of death are nutrition related. We need to eat more fiber, fish, poultry, and vegetables, and less red meat, sugar, and salt. Poorly nourished people succumb to stress quicker.

Rest and Relaxation

All of us need to relax. There are countless demands and stresses on us, more so than ever in this day in which we live. It is suggested that we set aside fifteen to twenty minutes a day, in addition to our exercise and personal devotional time, where we let all the stops out—no demands on us, and no decisions that have to be made. It might be playing with the dog. It might be playing with the children. It might be walking, listening to music, or working in the garden. It could be anything— as long as there are no demands and we are able to completely relax all our tense muscles.

It's also a good idea to plan a pleasant activity once a week that you look forward to—a little hope at the end of the week that kind of spurs you on. Most of us need something to look forward to, something we anticipate with joy and eagerness.

Don't forget, Christ is the greatest stress reliever there is, as he reminds us, "Come to Me, all you who labor . . . , and I will give you rest" (Matt. 11:28). We will not get rid of stress, but we do have a choice as to how we deal with it. We do not have to be its victim!

Reach Out to Others

Altruism, an unselfish concern for the welfare of others, is another essential ingredient to managing or reducing stress in our lives. It is impossible, as popularly attested today, to live entirely for yourself, giving no thought to others, and still be satisfied and content.

Our Lord Jesus taught, lived, and operated according to a completely opposite principle. He declared, "For even the Son of Man did not come to be served, but to serve. . . . Whoever wishes to save his life shall lose it, but whoever loses his life for My sake, he is the one who will save it" (Mark 10:45; Luke 9:24 NASB).

J. Sidlow Baxter calls it the "joy-secret of otherism." He writes,

In one of the bedrooms of a certain Christian home there hangs a little card which bears the words: THE SECRET OF JOY—God first, others next, self last. Is this indeed the secret of joy? Then most of us are sadly wrong. We think that joy comes by the reverse order; and it is this mistake which lies behind the worship of wealth, the passion for power, and the pursuit of pleasure. The first secret of joy lies in otherism—a going out of one's heart toward others.

Egoism is the supreme enemy of true joy. By many providences God seeks to break our egoism down. Indeed, the very relationships which condition human family life are meant to break our egoism down. Henry Drummond says, "A man cannot be a member of a family, and remain an utter egoist." Certainly the mother teaches the child; but in a far deeper way, is it not the child who teaches the mother? And the little one teaches nothing sublimer than just this very thing—otherism.

OTHERISM! Let the word burn into the mind. Joy is a will-o'-the-wisp to those who run after it; but in some self-forgetting hour when we are touched by another's need, and we sacrifice to give succor, we suddenly find our hearts aflame with a glorious joy that has come unsought! It is thus that we come to know a like joy to that of our dear Lord.[4]

PART 2

THE BATTLE
FOR THE MIND

10

Two Opposing Belief Systems

At this point you may want to ask: Since I have known Jesus Christ as my own personal Savior, he has brought me back into harmony with God, and, since I know that God has planned for my personal-circle longings to be satisfied with himself and I am complete in him, why, then, do I still have such longings? such cravings for love? such a sense of inadequacy? such feelings of worthlessness? Where does satisfaction begin? In the next favorable set of circumstances?

Why Does My Personal Circle Seem So Empty?

Shirley was asking that same question when she wrote,

I have always had a problem with self-image. Now that I'm thirty-five and have never married, I feel even more like a mis-fit. Recently I went to a special meeting at church, only to

*discover it was totally family oriented. That evening was dev-
astating to what was left of my self-worth.*

*All my adult life I have struggled to believe that Christ has a
place for me, a complete place, as a single. But that night I
drove away with a heavy weight of worthlessness.*

*I feel more like a wart than a part of my church body. And I
know other single women who have been stuck in activities
that were family oriented so often they could scream. How do
we fit in when we are left out so much? I desperately long to
belong!*

Is God really adequate, totally sufficient for Shirley's
personal satisfaction and contentment? That is, will he
fill her personal circle?

There's something else about the way God made us
that I believe will help us to understand ourselves and
the difficulty we sometimes have in receiving personal-
circle fullness.

The Mind under Attack: Genesis 1–3

Adam was not only created as a personal being with
longings, but he was also created with

a mind to think and know.
a will to decide and choose.
emotions to feel and enjoy.

Adam had a full personal circle (see figure 10.1). He had
total harmony with God as they walked and talked
together in the garden. He had total harmony with the
woman God had given to be his complement. He was
blessed with abundant physical provision in the garden.

Satan didn't like all this harmony and satisfaction.
Subtle and clever as he was, he knew just where to

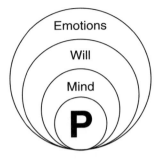

Figure 10.1

attack—the mind! His question to Eve was, "Has God indeed said, 'You shall not eat of every tree of the garden'?" (Gen. 3:1). (See figure 10.2.)

Eve answered on the basis of her belief system, which had been placed in her by God himself, "Yes, we may eat from all, except one. If we eat of that we will die" (see Gen. 3:2–3).

Satan kept chipping away at Eve's belief system: "Oh, no, you won't die. That's not really true. And besides, God is keeping back something good. All you have to do is eat of that tree and your life will be fuller, richer, more

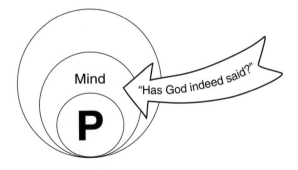

Figure 10.2

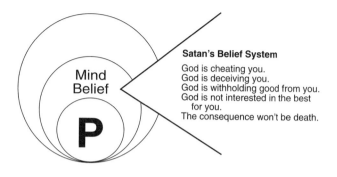

Figure 10.3

satisfying—your personal circle will be fuller" (see figure 10.3 and Gen. 3:4–5).

Now Eve is faced with two opposing belief systems: Satan's—based on untruth and lies; and God's—based on solid, eternal, unchanging truth (see figure 10.4).

Eve is forced to make a decision, a choice, with her will. After she had considered with her mind all the "new facts" (lies) Satan offered, with her will she chose to believe what Satan said and to go his way. Did eating of that tree suddenly bring more satisfaction and more harmony? Were things suddenly better?

Sin Ruins Personal-Circle Fullness

In that one simple act of disobedience sin entered the world and ruined the perfect personal-circle fullness Adam and Eve had been enjoying. And sin has ruined it for all of us since that time.

Now, like Eve, instead of being satisfied with God and what he is providing moment by moment, we are always looking beyond, looking away from what we have to what we might be missing; looking in the wrong direc-

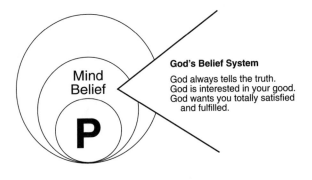

God's Belief System

God always tells the truth.
God is interested in your good.
God wants you totally satisfied
and fulfilled.

Figure 10.4

tion for what would bring satisfaction and what would quench our thirst.

Now, instead of contentment and peace, there is discontent, restless frustration, anxiety, guilt, and fear. Instead of being content with what we have or who we are, we are filled with discontent, dissatisfaction, and a restless desire for something more or different.

11

Broken Cisterns

There is an alternative to choosing personal-circle fullness in Christ. Instead of finding our deepest longings met and our needs satisfied in God himself, we turn the world upside down seeking that which will quench the God-implanted thirst for himself. We are on an endless search for something more or something different that we believe we must have in order to be satisfied, fulfilled, content, and at peace. Jeremiah painted a graphic picture of this constant reaching out to grasp after satisfaction.

> My people have committed two sins:
> They have forsaken me,
>   the spring of living water,
> and have dug their own cisterns,
>   broken cisterns that cannot hold water.
>
> Jeremiah 2:13 NIV

Two sins are named in this passage. First, humans have forsaken God, the spring of living water. They have deserted the One who can quench the thirst within, the One who alone can give true satisfaction. They have abandoned the One from whom love, acceptance, forgiveness, and strength flow. They have renounced the only One who can ultimately give personal-circle fullness—a full sense of unconditional love, worth, and competence.

Second, humans have dug their own cisterns—broken cisterns that can hold no water—to seek after other sources that they hope will quench their thirst for love, worth, and competence. A cistern is a reservoir or tank used for collecting and storing rainwater, in contrast to a stream of fresh, clean water flowing from a spring. Any person, circumstance, or thing can be turned into a broken cistern when we seek satisfaction from it, instead of from God himself. A disillusioned church member wrote,

I have been reaching out to the local church to meet my needs and I'm always disappointed. It's such an imperfect body. Sometimes I want to quit attending altogether. I see now that I am looking to my church, at least in some degree, to meet my personal-circle longings. If there are others in the church who are doing the same thing, it's no wonder we're disappointed in our church. Our focus is wrong. We are self-centered and incapable of ministering to others.

Personal-circle fullness does not mean a life of ease, a bed of roses, or skies that are always blue. It does mean having adequate resources to meet any circumstance because I have determined to believe that God himself, and what he chooses to provide at this moment, is all I need for peace and contentment at this moment.

If we think our peace is found in favorable circumstances, in other people's positive response to us, or in something that we do not have right now, our minds will dream up all kinds of broken cisterns.

- A mother kept reaching out trying desperately to find a husband for her unmarried daughter. A broken cistern.
- A young mother of two preschoolers thinks the grass was greener before her boys came along. She used to direct a camp every summer. Now summer comes and she stays in her own backyard lamenting, "If I could only break away from such confinement!" A broken cistern.
- A friend, whose faithful friend of many years rejects her, feels she must have that friendship back. A broken cistern.
- A wife, whose husband has rejected her for another lover, feels she must have him back to be happy. A broken cistern.
- A wife whose husband, a sex addict, has lied, deceived, and made her life difficult, says, "He must apologize." A broken cistern.
- A single woman thinks the only source of contentment and fulfillment is in a husband and family. A broken cistern.

Even though we should not reach out to broken cisterns for contentment, this does not negate the importance of balancing the truth by taking the responsibility to address the issue sometimes.

One woman thought she could never be happy until her separated parents were reunited.

My parents have been separated for two years. This has caused me more grief and pain than anything I have ever expe-

rienced. I have released my mother (who left my father) to God many times, only to find myself pulling her back again. Deep down I felt that my joy would never be complete until they were reunited.

What a relief to realize that my joy can be complete despite the outcome of their marriage because I can choose to believe that God is all I need. God has not, at this moment, chosen to heal this marriage; instead he has shown me that I can rest in his timing and his control.

With or without the healing of the marriage I can have joy and restfulness. God is faithful and I can trust him to bring about his purposes in my parents' lives. My emotions are slowly catching up to this truth. The pain is still present, but recognizing his control of the situation allows my joy to remain in spite of the pain.

Do you ever try to dig your own cisterns by reaching to get something for yourself that God isn't providing for you at this moment? It is so easy to "spend money for that which is not bread" when all the while the only true Bread of Life patiently waits to satisfy us with an abundance of peace—no monetary cost involved—just a surrendering of our will to his and a trusting in his love and goodness.

In looking away from God, humans create an emptiness and then go on searching on their own for something to fill that emptiness—for cisterns from which they can drink. I call it the greener-grass syndrome. "If only I had. . . . If only I didn't have. . . . If only. . . . if only. . . . if only. . . ."

Ho! Every one who thirsts, come to the waters;
And you who have no money come, buy and eat.
Come, buy wine and milk
Without money and without cost.
Why do you spend money for what is not bread,

And your wages for what does not satisfy?
Listen carefully to Me, and eat what is good,
And delight yourself in abundance.

Isaiah 55:1–2 NASB

What an infinite mistake to miss the fountain that is freely flowing to quench our thirst and to dig out broken cisterns that contain disappointment and despair. There is the cistern of pleasure, the cistern of wealth, and the cistern of human love, to name but a few. None of these, however, can fully satisfy the human soul. All cisterns dug at infinite cost of time and strength are treacherous and disappointing.

You who are weary, come back to God. Forsake the cisterns—the friendships, the idolatries, the sins that have alienated you from the Fountain of Living Water. Open your heart to him. Hear him say, "If anyone thirsts, let him come to Me, and drink" (John 7:37).

> I came to Jesus, and I drank of that Life-giving stream;
> my thirst was quenched, my soul revived, and I now
> I live in Him.[5]

12

THE GREENER-GRASS SYNDROME

We all want to be our own gods and choose the things, people, and events that we think will bring us satisfaction, fulfillment, and joy to fill our personal circle. We no longer trust God's judgment but set ourselves up as a wiser judge of what will satisfy. By our attitudes and actions we are saying, "I will go my own way. I know what is best."

The greener-grass syndrome starts with the personal-circle longings (see figure 12.1), then moves to the rationale—the beliefs, thoughts, and principles that control the mind. The choices that people make are based on those controlling principles.

Just as Eve did long ago, modern humans say, "I will use the mind that God has given me and decide what is best. Satan is right. If God really loved me, if he were really good, he would not withhold from me anything that seems good. God and what he has given are not

73

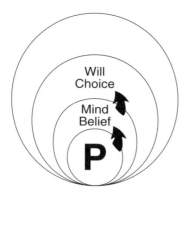

Figure 12.1

enough. I need something more, something different. I will go for it."

As a single I may say, "I would be much happier if I had a husband and children." So I go for it. My whole life centers on how I can connive and order my world until I get the thing my warped belief system has convinced me would satisfy my ultimate longings. Remember, the desire or need may not be wrong in itself, but when it takes on the strength of an inward demand, *I must have it to be happy,* we are exalting our wisdom above God's. All of us can relate to this drive to find satisfaction in something more or something different than what God has given us. Here are some examples people have shared with me.

I am very, very depressed. I've been dating this guy for seven years. He has promised me for five of those years that we would get married. At the present I have decided not to see him, but I'm miserable. Please help me! I have a job I like, but I need a husband, someone I can love and someone who will love me. I own a small house and it's very hard for a woman to do everything. And I'm so afraid of being alone forever.

This thing of being trapped in this house, having to take care of these three kids all day long, and then to have an insensitive husband come home and expect to be waited on is for the birds! I would be much happier if I got out and put my abilities to work in a more creative, fulfilling way. I'm going to go for it. After all, I have needs too. I need to hear something more than baby babble all day. I'll go for something more challenging and satisfying.

I'm sick and tired of living in this cracker box of a house. I'd be happier if I had more room, a bigger house with a bigger lawn in a nicer community.

If my husband (or friend) would just be more sensitive, more understanding, talk more (or talk less), then I'd be happy.

If only my gay child would turn around.

If only I weren't so shy. If I didn't have this temperament or if the people around me were different, then I could be a contented, satisfied person.

A dear friend was pouring out her heart to me again. We had gone over these same questions many times before, but she asked again.

Does this Christian life really work? If Christ is supposed to be concerned about me and meeting my needs, why doesn't he provide those things that will meet my needs? Why am I so lonely, so frustrated, so filled with unrest? Where is that peace and joy he promises? I read my Bible and pray regularly. I commit myself to him. I trust him. Why doesn't he deliver according to his promise?

I have such a craving for companionship, love, satisfaction, and purpose in life. I feel marriage would give this, but even though I've had some good opportunities, God has not unlocked my heart and directed my love to anyone I've met. I feel like a helpless victim of my intense desire to be loved by someone and to have acceptance and approval.

We talked and shared some Scripture together. After a while she was somewhat comforted. The next morning after her time with the Lord she wrote to me.

I just read a paragraph in one of my devotional books that really spoke to me regarding our talk last night:

Complaining can develop into a fine art! Some tarnished souls can look at any situation and tell you what is wrong with it. Such people are "walking minus signs." Unfortunately, a few of these sour spirits have joined our churches. They look as though they sucked lemons for breakfast. One of these saints is said to have lived complaining and died complaining. When he finally got to Heaven, his first comment was, "The halo don't fit!"[6]

I had to laugh because just prior to reading this I was again dealing with my never-ending attitude of complaint and dissatisfaction. I had just listed the ways the Lord had caused my cup to overflow. I realized that as he gave, I made it my business to pick and grumble over the imperfections rather than stand in awe of what he had given. How ungrateful I've been!

After two years without a church or fellowship with Christians, he gave me both. Was I happy? No, he didn't give me fellowship with people my age.

Then he gave me fellowship with people my age. But not enough of it and not often enough for me to be satisfied.

I had a good job that challenged my skills. But I wanted a "Christian" job. He gave me a Christian job. But then I wanted one more like the one I had before.

Then he gave me the wonderful privilege of having a very close friend. But I wanted more of her time—make that all of her time!

I have a wonderful, self-sacrificing roommate. But I want to live alone.

Get the picture? No matter how much the Lord gives, I'm never satisfied. If only I were married, but then it would be if only I had children, and then, if only they were potty trained, if only the children were grown, if only they'd get married, if only they'd give me grandchildren, if only, if only, if only! Where does satisfaction begin?

Where *does* satisfaction begin? Does it come in the next set of favorable circumstances? Why do you still have these deep longings? Why does your personal circle seem so empty at times? Why are you so discontent, always wanting something more, something different?

Very simply stated, your personal circle is empty because you have wrong beliefs. And your wrong beliefs lead you to make wrong choices about how to fill your personal-circle longings. You begin to dig out cisterns, cisterns that hold no water, cisterns that cannot possibly satisfy that deep longing, that inward demand.

So, what is the answer? We're going to look for some solutions by starting where Satan started with Eve. We're going after the real culprit: our belief system.

13

BUILDING OUR BELIEF SYSTEM

From the Scriptures we can see that our belief system is attacked by three corrupting influences—the flesh, the devil, and the world.

The Flesh

The flesh might be defined as the sinful element in man's nature. Even the believer is not free from the downward pull of the flesh, "On the one hand I myself with my mind am serving the law of God, but on the other, with my flesh the law of sin" (Rom. 7:25 NASB). The flesh has a bent toward selfishness and self-realization. Its tendency is self-centeredness rather than other-centeredness.

Our fallen nature reveals itself in this bent toward a self-sufficient, self-concerned, independent spirit with a determination to have our own way. The flesh as we have defined it here plays a major role in shaping what we believe about ourselves and what we believe about the way life should be lived. Its basic tenet is: Go to it. Decide what you want. Get what you want. Seek to satisfy your longings in any way you think they might be satisfied. "Every man did what was right in his own eyes" (Judg. 17:6 NASB).

The Devil

Satan himself puts thoughts in our minds that are contrary to God's thoughts. He is actively in the business of tempting us to doubt what God says, just as he tempted Eve. Satan's encounter with Jesus in the wilderness is case in point (Matt. 4:1–11). Satan was saying, "See—your Father is obviously not meeting your needs. Let me suggest a better way. Make the stones bread. Throw yourself down. Fall down and worship me." Each of Satan's statements was totally contrary to the Father's perfect plan for his Son.

Satan also uses people, sometimes close friends, as in the case with Peter and Jesus, to add the wrong ideas to our belief system.

> And Peter took Him [Jesus] aside and began to rebuke Him, saying, "God forbid it, Lord! This shall never happen to You." But He turned and said to Peter, "Get behind Me, Satan! You are a stumbling block to Me; for you are not setting your mind on God's interests, but man's."
>
> Matthew 16:22–23 NASB

The World

One mother said she spent seventeen years building godly values and principles into her daughter, who became a beautiful Christian woman in character and commitment to the Lord—until she went to the university. "That one year in the university seemed to wipe out everything we had taught her. However, prayer—many hours on my knees—and God turned her around."

The philosophy of the world today is a tremendously powerful influence in breaking down godly values and building a wrong belief system. But our major emphasis here will be our immediate personal world that is around each of us.

From our earliest moments outside our mother's womb you and I have been collecting beliefs and building a belief system. J. B. Phillips expressed the process so clearly in his version of Romans 12:2, "Don't let the world around you squeeze you into its own mold."

When a child enters life, he or she comes with two basic questions: Does anyone love me? and, Does anyone care about me, my pain, my need? Please show me that you're there, that you love me and care for me (see figure 13.1). Show me by touching me, holding me, talking to me, changing me, feeding me.

As a baby moves toward childhood, he or she begins to add another question: Can I do anything worthwhile? Notice that the three questions are related to the personal-circle longings, to the triad of personal needs. The events that happen in a baby's world, the things that are said to him, the attitudes communicated to her, are so significant because through these he or she is building a belief system.

A young pastor and his wife have three boys between five and nine years of age. Just this year a little girl was added to the family. They have been a camping family, and with three boys, they enjoyed setting up a tent and roughing it. Now just a few weeks ago they took their first camping trip with eight-month-old Ruth.

To keep her safe and close to them, they had her sleeping between them in their sleeping bag. About midnight they awoke. Ruth had thrown up—all over herself, her mother, and the sleeping bag. And the one thing they had forgotten to bring was a flashlight!

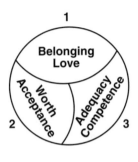

Figure 13.1

As they began to grope around to clean up the smelly mess, the mother turned to Ruth and in a gentle, loving tone said, "Dear Ruthie, we will never leave you nor forsake you."

What was the input into that little baby's belief system that moment as her parents calmly and willingly cleaned her up, cleaned up the stinky mess in the sleeping bag, and spoke such kind, reassuring words to her? Could she understand the words? Probably not. Could she sense accmeptance and love? Oh yes!

What might they have done instead? What could have been their attitude? What would that have done to Ruthie's belief system? Ruth's world around her was giving her good input at that moment, and she was building a stockpile of acceptance, affirmation, and self-esteem.

Feeding the Belief System

God designed the human family to be the children's environment—their own little world where they would be loved and cared for, where their needs would be met, and where loving parents would meet their human needs and model God's love, care, and value of them and

God's willingness and ability to help them in their times of need.

Parents whose personal circle is full and affirmed by each other can freely and unselfishly minister to the needs of their children, affirming their dignity as significant people. How comfortable! The children know they are loved and cared for. They're satisfied and content. Their three questions are being answered positively. They are getting good input into their belief system from the world around them. They're OK. They are wanted, loved, and cared for. They are respected as people with needs.

The attitudes and words of others toward us, as well as our interpretation of the events of our lives, have a profound effect on our belief system—for good or bad. When my brother repeatedly told me in our growing-up years, "If I couldn't sing any better than that, I sure wouldn't try," that's direct input! And it's not surprising I still struggle with a sense of inadequacy regarding singing.

How do you think a child would interpret words such as these?

> "You're so dumb!" (spoken with impatience and disgust)
>
> "Jesus doesn't like little boys and girls who . . ." (shouted in a threatening, scolding, rejecting, accusing tone of voice)
>
> "Can't you ever do anything right?" (screamed out with sarcasm for even the neighbors to hear)

One mother wrote to me about an incident that caused her to rethink the messages she was sending her son.

Our preschool son just recently found a bottle of permanent black ink on the road in front of our house. Naturally, out of sheer curiosity he opened it and decided that our front porch needed a new look. Well, now our white and gray porch is also black polka-dotted!

I was so angry with him. For days I kept reminding him how bad he was. And for days he wouldn't look at anyone. He just hung his head, afraid of what I might say next. When I saw how badly I was hurting him, and realized that a new coat of paint would hide his handiwork, I stopped picking on him and started forgiving. My little boy, with his very tender heart, has learned his lesson and, hopefully, I have learned mine and will keep my mouth shut while I repaint the porch.

From infancy and early childhood we have been recording positive and negative messages. If parents are cold and matter-of-fact, unable or unwilling to express affection, the child concludes that he is unlovely and unlovable. One person shared,

Whenever I would put my arms around my father and say "I love you," he would take my arms down and push me away out of awkwardness. It made me feel so alone and unwanted.

If parents react out of impatience with the child's slow learning of skills or habits, the child will feel he is a bother and think he is very inadequate. If the parent is irritated over the baby's middle-of-the-night needs or the child's slow learning of motor skills, the child will record negative messages about herself in response to these negative attitudes.

A censoring tone, a condescending manner, a disapproving facial expression, harsh, critical, overexaggerated words can easily cause the child to feel insecure, inadequate, and unloved.

Parents can destroy our confidence and hinder the development of our decision-making powers even after we are grown by simple words spoken with tones of disdain and ridicule.

> "You don't want *that* car! There's no way you can afford it."
> "You look awful in that suit! Why did you ever spend your money for it?"

It's not so much the nature and character of the event that happens to me, but my interpretation of the event and what I say to myself about the event that actually puts content into my belief system. This is true of my childhood experiences as well as the current events of my life. As you read the following true account, look for the assumptions and inferences about herself that resulted from Sara's interpretation of the events of her childhood.

I lived with my single mother until I was eight years old. She doted on me and probably spoiled me terribly. When I was seven, she married and my stepfather and I had some very bad scenes.

I was never told why I was put up for adoption a year later, but I assumed it was because I was a brat. I was so afraid of being rejected by my new family that I did everything I could to stay out of trouble and to please them. Whenever I did do something wrong and needed correction, I took the correction as rejection.

I internalized every single negative word that was said to me and had extremely bad periods of depression. I tended to feel that I was the cause of everything that went wrong in the adult world around me. It is hard even now not to blame myself for everything that goes wrong.

I came to know Christ fifteen years ago and am slowly choosing not to believe some of the negative things that came from my parents during my very sensitive childhood. This is hard to do because some of those offhand remarks stuck like glue in my mind. With God's Word taking the place of those bad words, I am becoming a healthier person. God has corrected many of these misbeliefs and healed many of the wounds.

We tend to feel that we are worthy or unworthy, adequate or inadequate, according to how we *think* other people feel toward us, so we need to discover our interpretation of the event. Then we need to ask, based on that interpretation, What am I telling myself about this event? What entry did I make into my belief system about me, about others, about God?

For example, the woman whose father pushed her away could ask: Was I really unlovable? Or was it just my father's awkwardness and inability to express love that made him push me away? Sara could ask: Was I put up for adoption because I was such a brat? Or were there other problems between my mother and my stepfather that made them unable to care for me?

In another case a young mother was worried and anxious about what people would think of her for having four children. As you read her story, try to answer these questions:

Why did she have feelings of shame and disgrace?
What were her wrong beliefs?
Where do you think she got those wrong beliefs?
How were they corrected?
What is the truth she should focus on and believe?

When I was expecting my fourth child I often had feelings of shame and disgrace when I was out in public. People would look at me and I would think, What are they thinking of me— pregnant and three children already?

Shortly after I delivered my baby I attended Verna's work-shops. When she shared about child acceptance, the Holy Spirit zeroed in on me. I knew I had rejected my children and had bitter thoughts about having four children.

The Lord showed me what a blessing and privilege it was that he gave them to me. I admitted my sin to him and was cleansed. Now I have a whole new outlook on my children. They truly are a gift from the Lord.

Our belief systems have been developing since our earliest moments of life. The world around us has been subtly squeezing us more and more into its own mold. But there's a better way—replacing Satan's lies with God's truth. How do we take an active role in this battle for the mind?

14

THE BATTLE
FOR THE MIND

We've talked in detail about the three belief systems battling for control in the believer. If we are committed to going God's way, then we need to take an active part in this battle for our minds in order to work with God in replacing our wrong beliefs with his truth. Before detailing how we can do this in specific situations, there are a couple of basics we must understand that underlie every misbelief that takes root in our minds.

First, we must recognize that the basic misbelief on which most other misbeliefs are attached is this: I need something more or different to have personal-circle fullness, that is, peace and contentment. Where did this misbelief come from? Why do I have such a strong tendency to believe and operate on this fallacy?

This misbelief is inherent in my fallenness. In my self-centeredness I grasp at satisfaction through things and people around me.

This misbelief is affirmed by the world. Everyone is out for Number One. The first consideration is my own needs. You—husband, wife, friend, mother, child—are in my world to meet my needs.

This misbelief has been reaffirmed by my interpretation of the events of my life. If I grew up in a permissive environment where selfishness was fostered and promoted, what else can I expect? I continue to have this same attitude of selfishness toward my spouse and my friends.

This misbelief has become a practiced lifestyle. I've assumed unconsciously that if my spouse or friend loved me, he or she would meet all my needs.

Second, because God's thinking is totally contrary to what I've been squeezed into thinking by the world around me I need to make a conscious decision, a definite declaration of faith: I choose to believe that God, and what he chooses to provide at this moment, is all I need. My personal circle is full.

So utterly simple, but so very difficult to appropriate. Perhaps we've had a soul struggle to come to this point, but we've made this declaration and we are committed to choosing personal-circle fullness as we have defined it here. Now we are ready to begin identifying and replacing our wrong beliefs with God's truth in specific situations. These thoughts can be a guide.

Emotions: God's Safety Valve

The consequences of the choice Eve made to believe Satan's lie rather than God's truth then reached into both her and her husband's emotions. Immediately after their wrong choice, "The eyes of both of them were opened" (Gen. 3:7), just as Satan had predicted. His method is to base his deceit on partial truth.

Adam and Eve felt guilty. They realized they were naked so they made fig-leaf aprons to cover up. Then they heard God coming. They felt more guilt, so they hid themselves from him among the trees. But God called Adam, "Where are you?" Fear entered. "I heard Your voice . . . and was afraid because I was naked; and I hid myself" (Gen. 3:9–10).

That sense of guilt and fear that Adam and Eve knew was another part of God's marvelous creation—a warning system, a safety valve God has built into us. Most of us will agree that our positive, good emotions are a God-given gift. They help us to enjoy life. But we may not have recognized that our wrong, negative emotions are also much of a gift, but for a different reason. They tell us that something is wrong and needs to be made right.

When I get angry (and I cannot justify my anger as righteous), that anger tells me that I have an inward demand that isn't being satisfied. The Bible tells us, "Be angry, and do not sin" (Eph. 4:26). J. B. Phillips gives us a checkpoint to help us discern if anger is sinful. "If you are angry, be sure that it is not out of wounded pride or bad temper."

In short, I get angry because I think things in my world are not working right and I choose to give way to a demanding spirit. I am blocked from getting my way, from getting what I call a need met. Inwardly I believe I have a right to have it my way. I believe something else needs to be added for personal fullness.

We hear much today about the value of getting in touch with our emotions. Is that a true statement? Yes, because destructive, wrong, negative emotions are a message from God to me. They are God's warning signals to steer me back on the right track. That destructive, bad emotion tells me something is wrong in my life. Scripture warns, "Do not let the sun go down on

your wrath, nor give place to the devil" (Eph. 4:26–27).
Satan rides in on anger, discouragement, and guilt.

A single mother writes of being freed from guilt.

I was carrying a lot of guilt. I've been worrying that Tanya
may resent me someday for having her as a single mother. Of
course I sinned, and I have groveled in that guilt for four years.
Now I finally realize that I'm forgiven! I'm no longer held in that
bondage of guilt, and I can now praise God for my beautiful lit-
tle girl.

Is guilt always a destructive emotion? It can be
destructive, but if we let it be a message from God, a
warning signal to lead us to confess sin and receive God's
full and free forgiveness, we have heeded the warning
of this marvelous built-in safety valve, our emotions,
and have been freed from the guilt.

Hear What I'm Saying to Myself

My thoughts are inner conversations with myself. We
find many references to this in Scripture.

He says to himself . . . (Ps. 10:6 NASB).

The fool has said in his heart . . . (Ps. 14:1).

Bless the Lord, O my soul! (Ps. 103:1).

If I listen to what I'm saying to myself, this will give me
some strong clues as to what is in my belief system.

As an adult, Elaine looked back at her childhood.

I see now that my family had a bent to be very impatient. We
never learned to listen patiently to each other and show inter-
est in what others were saying. I grew up with a real fear of

*talking to people because I was sure they would very quickly
get tired of listening to me as my family had.*

*Even now I usually say something in as short a way as pos-
sible so that people won't get tired of listening to me and turn
away in rejection. I tell myself that everyone listening to me is
as impatient as all of us in our family were. Growing up with
that attitude around me constantly has made me very insecure
in my conversational ability.*

What was Elaine saying to herself?

- People don't want to talk with me.
- I don't have anything worthwhile to say.
- I shouldn't talk much because no one wants to lis-
  ten to me.

Many of us do exactly as Elaine was doing. We par-
rot back to ourselves what was said or implied to us in
our childhood. It could be any one of thousands of
stored-up messages.

- They probably won't like me.
- I'm stupid; I can't do anything right.
- I'm not pretty and I can't sing. I'm useless.
- Church gatherings aren't for me. I'm too shy.
  People don't want to talk to me. They're just inter-
  ested in their own friends.

Having said these things to ourselves for years, the
grooves in our belief system are deep. Because of this
we tend to greatly exaggerate and wrongly interpret
people's reactions to us and misinterpret their thoughts
about us. Debasement becomes an easy habit. We are
constantly thinking, *This is awful. Terrible. Horrible. A
disaster! It's wretched! I'm stupid. A failure. Miserable.
Worthless!*

It is often not easy to recognize and admit what we're telling ourselves. Sometimes other people might even need to help us realize what we're saying to ourselves. But we do need to get in touch with our inner conversations, our self-talk.

Judge My Belief

Since my self-talk may or may not be true and accurate, I need to make a judgment as to whether or not what I believe is a true belief (based on Scripture) or a misbelief. One way I can check this out is by asking myself, Am I saying that I must have something more or something different in order to have my personal circle full and to experience contentment and peace? What are we doing when we insist we must have something else in order to know and enjoy personal-circle fullness? We are afflicted with the greener-grass syndrome. We are digging our own cisterns, broken cisterns that can hold no water and thus never satisfy our insecurities and deep longings.

We can also ask ourselves, Am I exaggerating the situation? Have I debased myself to the point where I can no longer see things as they really are? As I endure a social gathering feeling unwanted, uninteresting, and uninvolved, can I realistically judge my tendency to debase myself? Instead, I can say:

> "I may feel like a misfit, but in truth my personal circle is full, and I am complete in Christ."
> "I may feel uncomfortable in this group, but I'm accepted in Christ!"
> "I may feel I said the wrong thing, but I have working within me the power of the Holy Spirit and he promises to make me competent. I trust him."

Paul declared in the midst of his trials, "I believe God that it will be just as it was told me" (Acts 27:25). This was his statement of truth. The writer of Hebrews affirmed that because God has said, "I will never leave you nor forsake you," he himself could boldly say, "The Lord is my helper; I will not fear . . ." (Heb. 13:5–6). This was his statement of faith and truth.

We must speak truth to ourselves. This truth is found in God and in his Word. Where we have been telling ourselves an untruth—literally a lie—we need to declare it a misbelief and state clearly and precisely what the truth is in regard to that situation. Instead of letting my misbelief lead me to reach out and dig another broken cistern, I need to replace that misbelief with a fresh affirmation of truth and wrap it around my own commitment.

A disillusioned wife wrote,

Ten years ago I married a Christian man with the desire and expectation that we would serve the Lord together—loving him with all our hearts, loyal to him above everything else. My husband was not the man I thought I had married. The Lord was not and still is not first in his life.

Oh, don't get me wrong—my husband says he loves the Lord and wants to obey him, but not with the deep love and dedication that I wanted for us. For ten years I've prayed that the Lord would give me the desires of my heart. I have everything most people long for—two wonderful boys, a stately home with a beautiful yard, close friends, and a good church. Yet, I'd rather have a shack, no money, and a husband totally given over to the Lord.

Until today at the workshop, I didn't realize I had bitterness toward the Lord for not giving me my deepest desires. I saw what I had been saying to myself: To enjoy personal-circle fullness I have to have a more dedicated husband. Now my statement of truth about the situation goes something like this: "Thank

you, Lord, for your sovereignty. I believe you draw to yourself
for service those whom you will. Your way is perfect and you are
in control of our lives. I choose to believe that you and what you
provide are enough to fill my personal circle. I praise you now for
the things you have graciously chosen to provide—a husband
who knows you and two children with whom I can teach and share
my love for you."

We refute wrong thinking and unwholesome inner
conversations by putting the event, the person, and the
circumstance within the circle of God's all-sufficient
grace. As I rest in his presence and believe his promises,
he will meet me there and give me a new perspective
(acceptance of the will of God) and a new attitude (contentment and peace).

I must learn to relate this present circumstance to
God, stating with confidence that

> God is in control.
> God loves and cares for me.
> God has promised to work all things for my good.
> God will never fail.

Continually Refute Contrary Thoughts

It takes discipline to do this. It's the discipline of bring-
ing every thought into captivity and making it obey
Christ, making it yield to God's truth (see 2 Cor.10:5). It
helps to have some systematic method to retrain our
wayward thought patterns.

One possible method is to immediately say the word,
Stop! when the unwanted thought comes as an intruder.
Say it either aloud or to yourself, but say it, and say it
with authority as a command. Then turn your thinking
to something else—state your declaration of faith, quote

Scripture, sing a song, pray for someone, count your blessings, plan your next meal, make a phone call. Another method is to take a 3" x 5" card. On one side write, "The lie is————." On the other side make a statement of truth specifically related to you and your situation. You may want to add a Scripture verse related to the topic. Keep your card handy and each time you need to, refer to it. Declare the untruth a lie, make your statement of truth, and say the verse. Memorize the statement and the verse.

Yet another possible method is the rubber-band-around-the-wrist idea to stop unwanted thoughts. When you begin to think a wrong thought, rather lightly—not cruelly—snap yourself with the rubber band and say aloud or think, "Stop thinking that thought." Then replace that wrong thought with truth—a statement, a Bible verse, or a song that counters or contradicts the lie.

Devise a method to fit your own special need, as Carla did.

Two years ago I fled from a very bad relationship the day before the wedding. I came away with a lot of guilt for letting it go so far and for all the heartache I caused so many people. In the months of readjustment I had to learn to accept God's forgiveness or my guilt would have destroyed me. I made a sign for the foot of my bed with the word forgiven written on it. I meditated on that until I had finally accepted it as fact.

These are helpful ways to renew the mind and transform living, as Romans 12:2 commands us. Choose or create a method most suitable to you and your need.

Prayer is an integral part of the above steps, but it is so important that we must see it as a separate step also. In Ephesians 6:18 we are told that when the armor is all in place, that's not enough. Then comes "prayer . . . with all perseverance . . . for all the saints."

We should avail ourselves of all the help at our disposal, but all the gimmicks, all the understanding we gain, even all the armor, will be worthless unless we are relying on the Holy Spirit to empower us (see Zech. 4:6).

Regularly Feed My Belief System on the Truth of God

I must daily attend to my personal circle and let God fill it afresh with new awareness of himself—who he is, his presence, his nearness, his promised provision for all my need, his grace, and his adequacy. Make it the first business of your day.

We must always be ready to combat the lies in our minds with the truth of God's Word. To do this we must make some effort to put the Word in. My realization of personal-circle fullness doesn't happen because I declare it so. God has made the provision; that's an unchanging fact. But I need to let him refresh my awareness of that fact and reaffirm it in my belief system through his Word. I also need to reaffirm it myself by my own commitment and choice of his Word and his ways.

I can so easily think I'm helplessly dry and thirsty when the Fountain of Living Water is there all the time and I just haven't chosen to drink from him.

15

How to Cope with Pain and Suffering

There is no magical formula for dealing with the difficult times of our lives. In fact, all that we have said in the previous fourteen chapters relates directly to coping with suffering. The more we have practiced our basic premise in little everyday pains and sufferings the better we will cope with the heavy suffering that may enter our lives. That basic premise, again (see figure 15.1), is that in every situation of life I must

Choose to believe
that God himself,
and what he chooses to provide
at this moment,
is all I need.

Figure 15.1

Against that backdrop we relate these basic principles to those who are going through a dark valley.

Realize God Is in the Situation

We must begin with a realization of God and a positive statement of faith: God is. He is here in my situation. He is good. He is in control. He is caring and loving and powerful enough to change things if that would be the very best for me.

We must accept the situation as from a loving Father's hand, believing it is his appointment at the present time. Refuse to demand something different or something more, though you greatly desire it and earnestly request it in prayer to your Father.

F. B. Meyer notes that Jesus' peace was based on such an acceptance. "The secrets of Jesus were the perpetual presence of God in his soul, and his never-faltering faith in the loving, careful providence of God in all the experiences of his chequered life."[7] Suffering is the common lot of all. Even Jesus "learned obedience from the things which He suffered" (Heb. 5:8 NASB).

Compare Your Self-Talk with God's Truth

What are you saying to yourself about God? Be honest with yourself. Are you entertaining any thoughts like these?

> God doesn't know or care about me.
> He can't do anything for me.
> The situation is impossible.

If those are your inner conversations, you need to correct those wrong thoughts with the clear truth of God's Word. Check out Exodus 33:14, Psalm 125:2, Isaiah 63:9,

Romans 8:38–39, 1 Corinthians 1:9, 2 Corinthians 9:8, Hebrews 4:15, and 1 Peter 5:7.

A second checkpoint is to ask what you are saying to yourself about yourself. Discover and admit any misbeliefs, such as:

I'm not good enough to have God's blessing.
God is punishing me.

Pain and suffering may be the inevitable result of sin, or God may use it to correct you, but he never uses it to punish you.

Your misbeliefs about yourself must be corrected by refuting them with Scripture—internalizing, accepting, and believing God's truth. Check out Isaiah 43 and Hebrews 12:1–13.

Declare Your Belief in Truth

Concerning suffering, or anything else in life that is not pleasant to us, we have a choice to make. Our choice can be either an attitude of acceptance, "Behold, the maidservant of the Lord! Let it be to me according to your word" (Luke 1:38); or it can be an attitude of resistance, "God forbid it, Lord!" (Matt. 16:22 NASB) or "Not so, Lord" (Acts 10:14).

If we choose the way of acceptance, our declaration of faith can be the now familiar, "Lord, I choose to believe your grace is sufficient for me. I choose to believe that you yourself and what you choose to provide at this moment are all I need. My personal circle is full." Acting with the will against all contrary feelings, repeatedly choose to believe God's truth in the midst of this suffering. "Thank you, Lord, that your ways are perfect. You make my way perfect" (see Ps. 18:30, 32).

Stand in Abraham's shoes as, against all hope, he believed. "He did not waver in unbelief, but grew strong in faith, giving glory to God, and being fully assured that what He had promised, He was able also to perform" (Rom. 4:20–21 NASB).

However, choosing to act with the will over the emotions is not the same as denying or suppressing the emotions. The same God who says, "Trust me," also says, "Pour out your heart before me" (see Ps. 62:8). We can trust him with our questions, our struggles, our grief, even our hostile, bitter feelings. Psalm 31 is a beautiful expression of the balance between feelings and faith. You may want to use it as your heart's cry to the Lord concerning your current situation.

Choose an appropriate method to rehearse God's truth; see the suggestions in chapter 14. Keep at it until you are finally able to declare, "It is good for me that I was afflicted, that I may learn Thy statutes" (Ps. 119:71 NASB).

Believe in God's Purpose

Choose to believe that God has a purpose in permitting this present suffering. Count on the afterward. He will bring good from it (Heb. 12:11). There is no such thing as chance in our lives. Dare to believe in God and trust his good purposes. His purpose includes personal learning and growth for you and an enlarged ministry to others. He desires

> that you might draw closer to him, know him better, and receive more of his comfort.
> that you might learn significant lessons of empathy, patience, hope, faith, submission.
> that your character might be refined.
> that you might be better able to minister to others.

Check out 2 Corinthians 1:3–7, James 1:2–4, 1 Peter 1:6–7, and 1 Peter 5:10.

Amy Carmichael tells of an experience when Andrew Murray of South Africa was in England taking part in various conventions. At one time they were both guests in the same house. Then something painful happened to Dr. Murray. Miss Carmichael records how he met the painful experience.

> He was quiet for a while with his Lord, then he wrote these words for himself:
> "First, He brought me here, it is by His will I am in this strait place, in that fact I will rest.
> "Next, He will keep me here in His love, and give me grace to behave as His child.
> "Then, He will make the trial a blessing, teaching me the lessons He intends me to learn, and working in me the grace He means to bestow (intends for me).
> "Last, in His good time He can bring me out again, how and when He knows.
> "Let me say I am here,
> 1. By God's appointment
> 2. In His keeping
> 3. Under His training
> 4. For His time."[8]

Let your suffering make you more alert to opportunities to minister to others. Take the opportunities and pray for more! You are no doubt now more sensitive to the feelings, fears, and weaknesses of those who suffer. You can share the hope God has given you. You can pray for them with deeper understanding.

A friend wrote,

This past summer has been the most difficult period of my entire life. God has brought some deep, painful, personal suf-

fering into my life. I sometimes despaired of physical life or of sanity, feeling I couldn't bear it.

But the Lord spoke to me very clearly that he had brought this circumstance into my life, and was calling on me for a deeper level of surrender. He asked me to accept the pain and embrace the brokenness, instead of fighting it or being swallowed in self-pity.

You know, I had asked to be made like Jesus, no matter what the cost! Ouch! So I have a great measure of peace, although there is still anguish and pain. I look forward to God's redemption of this circumstance in my life after I have gone through the fire. I have been deeply shattered, but the Lord has called me to minister to deeply shattered people.

Our world is full of suffering, comfortless people. It may be physical pain or soul agony. In either case the pain is real and the suffering is a fiery ordeal. It may come in the form of rejection by a mate or a dear friend. It may come through loss, loneliness, or the grief of death or divorce. It may come through a bodily ailment or infirmity. It may come through the bad behavior of children.

No matter how deep the valley or long and dark the tunnel, our greatest comfort is to know that God is here. He has a divine purpose and he is carefully watching for the moment when suffering has done its work and he can remove it (see Ps. 119:67, 71, 75, 91).

16

THOSE UGLY GREMLINS

All of life is one change after another from the cradle to the grave. We just get through one change and we're met with another. We cry with the song writer, "Change and decay in all around I see."[9] Some are small daily changes—the meeting is canceled, the washing machine breaks, the boss moves you to third shift, Billy cuts his lip and has to have stitches. Some are pleasant, eagerly anticipated changes—marriage, the birth of a child, graduation, a promotion, or a holiday. Some are traumatic, devastating, or confusing—retirement, the inability to have children, the unplanned-for child, unemployment, financial loss, career change, roommate change, new school, schooling at home, loss caused by natural disasters, trouble with the boss, conflict with the organist, and disagreement with the pastor. On and on we could go.

Why do we find it so hard to cope with change in our lives? It goes right back to the way we were made. We are made with the need for deep, intimate fellowship with God and with other human beings and the need for a life of meaning and purpose. During the changes in our lives something significant happens to our human relationships and to our sense of meaning and purpose in life. Each event brings a varying degree of loss. When relationships are affected, your circle of support gets smaller. When uncertainty comes, our sense of purpose in life is diminished.

Making a Declaration

Growing older is a process of change that has its own set of multiple losses, transitions, and adjustments. Again there are losses in relationships and in a sense of meaning and purpose in life.

One dear seventy-two-year-old lady (we'll call her Jo) shared some of her feelings, anxious thoughts, and fears and how she handled them. She wrote this beautiful declaration of commitment and faith.

My dear heavenly Father, how can I ever express how grateful I am for your great care over me through the years—for the loving lessons you have taught me, for the scrapes you have averted by your loving care, for my wonderful husband and three fine sons, for my two daughters-in-love (that's what we call them), and for our three beautiful grandchildren. You have been so good.

Why then, Lord, do these ugly gremlins come into my thinking from time to time? I worry about losing this wonderful husband that you have given me. How could I ever survive without him if he is taken before me? Will I have to suffer a long illness before you take me home? What if I end up in a rest home? Life seems so pathetic there. What if I become senile? I want so much to be alert and able to worship you to the end.

There now, I've verbalized them! Those ugly gremlins! Lord, forgive me for even allowing myself to think this way. I now commit all these worries about old age to you. I reaffirm my belief that you are the Blessed Controller of all things. I need not worry about my old age.

I will claim the promise that you have given me in Psalm 92:13–14, where you say that I am planted in the house of the Lord, and I will flourish in your courts. I shall still bring forth fruit in my old age and shall ever be full of sap and green to show that you are upright. You are my Rock and there is no unrighteousness in you.

Each time one of these fears comes up I will go back and review this commitment until I have peace. I can trust you with my old age. I praise you, Lord!

Whether our change points are pleasant or devastating, small or traumatic, we need to do exactly what Jo has done in regard to growing older.

First, Jo focuses on her blessings, not her adversities or trials. She focuses on the goodness and the faithfulness of the Lord to her throughout her past life. She is grateful for what she has and expresses her thanks instead of groaning about what she does not have.

Second, Jo faces the ugly gremlins that come into her thinking from time to time. She enumerates her worrisome thoughts, her wrong beliefs, and her "what-ifs."

Third, Jo takes responsibility for indulging in wrong beliefs and worrisome thoughts. "Forgive me for allowing myself to think this way," she prays. Then she doesn't bother herself anymore about them. Having received God's forgiveness they are gone and forgotten—no guilt harassment!

Fourth, Jo deliberately and decisively hands the worrisome circumstances over to the Lord and makes a statement of belief based on truth. "I reaffirm my belief that you are the Blessed Controller of all things and I need not worry about my old age."

Fifth, Jo states and claims some of the promises of God as they relate to her need and her renewed commitment to the Lord.

Sixth, Jo states that each time one of these fears comes up, she will go back and reaffirm her commitment until she has peace. It will be an action of her will even if her emotions do not feel trusting and fearless.

Seventh, Jo is reaching out to others. She is not just sitting back to see what old age will bring to her, hoping she can cope, but she is looking away from herself to see the needs of others. She is doing some significant things to help them in a vital way. She is doing something about her need to still be useful and make a significant impact on her world.

In the postscript of her letter she wrote:

I have an Enriched Living cassette program going in my home. We had so many in our neighborhood who wanted to attend that we have one in the morning and one in the afternoon each Wednesday. We are anticipating two more classes through our church starting next week. A pastor's wife called me for information last week. Today she told me they plan to start some cassette classes in their church in January. I feel this is one way in which God is using me in our little town.

This simple but highly significant ministry is making an impact for God on her neighborhood. A by-product for Jo is a settled sense of usefulness.

I have detailed Jo's steps to contentment, peace, and a sense of purpose for two reasons. All of us are growing older and will have this same need to take these steps sometime in our lives. She acted wisely. We would do well to follow her example.

Second, the steps she took paralleled so perfectly and describe so specifically the steps outlined for you in chapter 14. These are the basic steps that all of us need to take in regard to change in our lives. We have to deal ruthlessly with our wrong thoughts and affirm that we will trust in God.

Always, always in the midst of changes, trying times, frustrations, anxieties, distresses, or fears, we need to relate the situation to the Lord, examine our own thoughts, identify those that are contrary to truth, correct them with truth, and put our case into God's hands. We must trust him, anchoring ourselves in him, his character, and his promises. We must choose to believe that God himself, and what he is providing at this moment, is all we really need.

We need to ask ourselves some hard questions and answer with a clear yes or no.

- Is God really in control of this event?
- Is this catastrophe an exception to his loving control?
- Is God really good?
- Is he actually interested in my best interests?
- Is his grace totally adequate for me at this time, in this place?
- Has he been faithful in the past? Will his faithfulness continue?
- Will I trust him now in this situation?

> Test me, O LORD, and try me,
> examine my heart and my mind;

for your love is ever before me,
  and I walk continually in your truth.
                              Psalm 26:2–3 NIV

In part 3 and part 4 we will be dealing with two of the most insidious misbeliefs our society is plagued with today. If we let the world around us squeeze us into its mold and believe these misbeliefs, we will be robbed of peace. We will experience more stress and less peace instead of less stress and more peace. We will be filled with anxiety and hurt and we will experience stress overload.

God's plan is that we settle the basic issue of "peace with God" (Rom. 5:1), and the "peace of God" (Phil. 4:7), as we have outlined in some detail in chapters 1–16. Then, instead of selfishly settling in to merely enjoy our contentment, we need to remember we are here to reach out to others to help them in their need.

PART 3

MISBELIEF #1:

I MUST DEMAND PAYMENT FROM MY DEBTORS

17

FORGIVE
YOUR DEBTORS

Several years ago, we were purchasing a large piece of equipment. After checking to see what several companies offered, we found only one that met our needs. Over the weeks that I talked with the salesman, he raised the price of the product three thousand dollars from what he had led us to believe it would cost.

I began to churn on the inside. It was also time for me to leave on a trip—to go out and teach people how to find Christ sufficient for the daily nitty-gritty. I didn't have time for a problem like this! To me, the whole thing was obviously unfair and totally ridiculous. Prices hadn't gone up that much. I wasn't going to let him get away with it! I tried hard to help him see that he had previously implied that the price would be three thousand dollars less, but he held firm. Our choice was clear: We could either buy the equipment at his inflated price or not buy it at all. We were hung because that machine

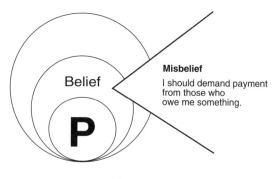

Figure 17.1

was the only one that met our need and we needed it right away. I had also learned that he had dealt deceptively with a number of other customers.

I really had to work this one out before the Lord. As I read the Psalms, I would write this man's initials by some of the verses, claiming that God was in control. As I rested the case with the Lord, believing God could and would handle the outcome, he worked my heart into freedom.

If he wanted me to waste three thousand dollars of our good money—no of *his* good money—in this unfair deal, that was his business and I would have to trust.

I made one final appeal to the salesman, but to no avail. There was no way he would change, but since I had turned it all over to the Lord, I had peace in the midst of the unfairness and the loss.

About that time I was also working on this book. I planned to include some of the worldviews that we can so easily get sucked into even as Christians. One of those worldviews goes something like figure 17.1.

In contrast, the truth of God is so simply stated in Matthew 6:12: Forgive your debtors (see figure 17.2).

So I talked to the Lord. "Lord, if I'm to teach this to the women, then I want to be sure that there's no one in

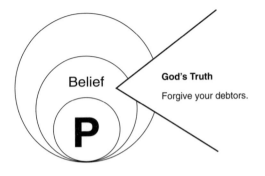

Figure 17.2

my life's circle who I think owes me something and inwardly I'm demanding payment. Lord, do I have any debtors that I haven't forgiven?"

Immediately this salesman's name came to my mind, and I reasoned with the Lord, "Lord, remember, I took care of that. See right here, Lord, in my Bible—all these verses I have marked with his name."

And then I remembered someone had recently told me that his business was not going well. Inwardly I was thinking, *He really needs to learn some lessons! I'm glad the Lord is beginning to give attention to that need.*

Just then the Lord spoke to my heart, "When you think of him and his hard time in sales, do you wish him well?" I hadn't wished him well at all. I had wished him ill. My attitude was to be glad for his misfortune because I thought he needed to learn a lesson.

This misbelief had taken root in my mind and inwardly I was demanding payment for something I felt the salesman owed me. He was my debtor. He owed me a debt of justice and fairness that he hadn't paid. I needed to forgive my debtor.

"Lord, forgive me. I haven't really forgiven my debtor."

18

WE ARE DEBTORS TO GOD

We are debtors primarily to God. Oh, how much we owe him! We can never pay it. The parable in Matthew 18 of the slave who owed his master ten thousand talents gives a picture of what that debt is like. But a picture, however strong, is never as strong as the truth it portrays.

What we owe God is like having a ten-million-dollar debt when eighteen cents a day is the wage. We can't repay. It's impossible! It would take 55,555,555 days or 152,207 years, working every day. It is impossible to pay! Likewise, we can never pay the debt we owe to God.

The good news is this: The debt to God has been paid in full—not revised, not reduced, but canceled! Forgiven! Removed! Jesus Christ paid the full penalty for all my sins when he died on the cross.

> For He [God] made Him [Jesus], who knew no sin to be sin for us, that we might become the righteousness of God in Him (2 Cor. 5:21).

As far as the east is from the west, so far has He removed
our transgressions from us (Ps. 103:12).

"Come now, and let us reason together," says the LORD,
"though your sins are like scarlet, they shall be as white
as snow; though they be red like crimson, they shall be
as wool" (Isa. 1:18).

God has forgiven us and canceled our certificate of debt
because of the work of Christ on the cross.

And when you were dead in your transgressions and the
uncircumcision of your flesh, He made you alive
together with Him, having forgiven us all our transgressions, having canceled out the certificate of debt . . .
which was hostile to us; and He has taken it out of the
way, having nailed it to the cross.

Colossians 2:13–14 NASB

Make a Definite Transaction with God

I don't have to pay my debt for sin. It's canceled! It
has been paid by another. But I do have to give personal
acknowledgement that Jesus Christ paid my debt of sin,
and I do have to make a definite transaction with God
based on these facts. I do this by committing myself to
him and by receiving Christ as my personal Redeemer
and Savior (see John 1:12).

If you have never done this, right at this moment you
can, by faith, receive him by praying, "Lord Jesus, I
know I am a sinner. I thank you that you died on the
cross for my sins. You have paid my sin debt in full. I
receive you now as my Savior and my Lord. Thank you
that I am forgiven and I am your child."

After we receive him, the only debt we have as God's
children is a debt of love, a debt of gratitude that we

want to pay. But how? How do we go about paying such a debt of gratitude to God for so great a salvation that has resulted in

our becoming his children?
our being free from the penalty and guilt of sin?
our enjoying his presence and power day by day?
the assurance of living eternally with him?

The song writer asserted, "Drops of grief can never repay the debt of love I owe."[10] So how can we pay our debt of gratitude to him? He says we can pay it by loving others. "Inasmuch as you did it to one of the least of these My brethren, you did it to Me" (Matt. 25:40).

It's as though God is saying, "The only debt you owe me is to love me and to show my love to others by loving them for me. That's all I want, nothing more. Love others just as I have loved you. Forgive others just as I have forgiven you."

God's Command to Love

Romans 13:8 teaches that we are not to stack up other kinds of debts toward one another, but we do owe a debt of love to each other. "Owe nothing to anyone except to love one another" (NASB).

What are some of the elements of love? That is, specifically what do we owe each other?

Fair treatment	Patience
Honor, Respect	Tolerance
Encouragement	Faithfulness
Understanding	Forgiveness
Affirmation	Kindness
Acceptance	Gentleness
Attention	Interest

...iis, and much more, is included in the many commands of Scripture to love one another and to build up one another (Prov. 10:12; Matt. 19:19; John 15:12; Rom. 12:9; 1 Cor. 13:4–7; Col. 3:12, 14; 1 Thess. 5:11).

Ephesians 4:32 gives a simple, but potent three-point summary of what it means to love, "And be kind to one another, tenderhearted, forgiving one another, just as God in Christ also forgave you." We owe each other love, and if we're honest, we'll have to admit that we haven't paid the debt of love as we ought.

We have seen that God has created us with deep, legitimate needs, longings, and desires that can only ultimately be satisfied by God himself. Yet, he has also chosen to use other people in our world to meet or affirm those needs on a human level.

Lana told how other Christians had disappointed her.

I came from Brazil fifteen years ago to make this country my home. Praise God I found Christ here! My mother died last year, leaving me in big financial trouble and completely alone. She was my best friend and I was devastated. I had a lot of resentment against Christians at that time. I was so alone and they didn't seem to understand that I needed them more than ever. Listening to you has helped me understand that I must forgive them for not caring for me during that difficult time.

Many are not paying what they owe us. We are all imperfect and fallen people in an imperfect and fallen world. And there is a lot of selfishness and failure to love. If others do not pay the debt of love they owe us, it is a wrong that causes us hurt. A God-created need in us has not been met by the other person, as God planned, and a legitimate hurt is the result.

Some parents have not paid what they owe to their children. They should have paid in a little more patience, a little more understanding, a little more respect, a little more time; but they didn't.

Some friends have not given others the attention, the understanding, the encouragement, and the purity they owe. They are debtors.

Some mates have not given their spouse the love, respect, faithfulness, and forgiveness they owe as marriage partners.

Some children have not given the love and honor they owe to their parents.

These all are debtors to the other. Instead of paying the debt of love they owe, they have at times given insult, disrespect, insensitivity, hate, and even abuse. This causes deep hurt and much pain. It creates distance, alienation, and separation in relationships because a basic God-given need is not being met as God planned. The key issue is not that I have been hurt, but how I respond to those who hurt me.

Responding to Those Who Hurt Me

When someone does not pay the debt of love they owe me, the hurt I feel is not wrong in itself. The wrong comes when I so easily let that hurt slide into resentment and bitterness toward the one who was the instrument of pain. I may also nurse the hurt into self-pity. I think, *Someone owes me something and did not pay. I don't like it! They must pay. They owe me time, friendship, acceptance, affirmation, justice, purity, and respect, and they haven't paid. I demand payment!*

Too frequently our human response is a desire to teach those who wrong us a lesson, which we think they should have learned long ago anyway. And in so many cases we are eager and ready to help God teach it to them! We may even rather secretly hope that some misfortune will come to them. Or, if we hear that a calamity has come to them we may think, *Well, they're finally getting what they deserve!*

What are your deep, inward thoughts or attitudes toward the person who failed you—the one who owed you respect and fairness, and didn't pay? Do you have a gleeful, vengeful feeling, or a merciful, compassionate, and prayerful attitude? In other words, do you secretly wish them ill? Or, do you wish them well? If you secretly wish them ill, then you have resentment in your heart. You're holding them as your debtor. You feel they must pay for their wrong behavior. You will not forgive them for the hurt they caused you. You put conditions on your forgiveness. You will not forgive them unless or until they change their behavior, apologize, and acknowledge how deeply they hurt you.

Resentment Has Power to Destroy

A hurting wife wrote me about how resentment almost destroyed her marriage.

For many, many years our home has been a battleground. My temper, my frustrations at not reaching the perfection I expected from myself, and my guilt over situations that happened to me as a nine-year-old, have all taken their toll on our family relationships. Six months ago my husband served me with separation papers. The hurt was devastating. I wanted to die! Instead, with the help of friends I was able to reach out to God and pray for his strength and love.

Shortly after the papers for separation were completed, my husband asked me to forgive him. "Let's try again," he said. I could not forgive him for the deep hurt I felt he had dealt me. Only after working hours and hours with my pastor and repeat-

edly going through the steps to forgiveness, was I able to say, "Yes, I forgive you."

Though we still have some shaky times, we are together. And resentment has not undermined what God wants to do to heal our marriage.

19

WHO ARE MY DEBTORS?

Remember, no matter how deep or how painful the hurt, the thing that has power to destroy us and keep God from healing those hurts is our resentment, our unforgiving spirit. We must choose to forgive our debtors! To do this we must first recognize who we are holding as debtors.

Spouse

Husbands and wives are to pay the debt of love to each other. God planned for them to unselfishly give to the needs of the other. He planned for them to

be committed and faithful to each other.
respect and affirm each other.
understand, comfort, and encourage one another.
stand by each other in times of failure, grief, or loss.

121

Instead, there has often been insult, lack of compassion, misunderstanding, and unfaithfulness. The result is intense pain. Resentment is fostered and grows. There is the inward demand, *He owes me this,* or the inward anguish, *I can't bear this any longer.*

Wives, husbands, pinpoint what it is you feel your spouse owes you. What is it that bugs you about him or her? What expectations do you have that your spouse is not meeting? What promises has your spouse made that he or she is not living up to? What advice does your spouse give others that is not followed in your own home?

One wife wrote to me about forgiving her spouse.

My husband had been involved with another man before we married and I could not get past this. I could not forgive him. It affected our intimate relationship and eventually he drifted away from God. When I realized I hadn't put this problem in God's hands, I came to the point of deliberately relinquishing my husband to God. That very day I was immediately able to forgive him and love him unconditionally. One year later we went to a marriage retreat and it wasn't long until he made a new commitment to Christ.

Husbands and wives, choose to forgive your debtor spouse.

Former Spouse

When your former spouse spends money on himself and your children go without, will you cancel the debt he owes you? When *your* car breaks down and your son reports on his recent ride in his mom's new BMW—will you choose to forgive your debtor?

Will you choose to forgive your ex-spouse for

turning away from you?
being unfaithful?
not paying what he owes financially?
being so insensitive?
taking advantage?
the way he or she is so unreasonable about the
children?

A wife wrote to me about her own experience forgiving a former spouse.

My ex-husband and I were married for twenty-five years. We were both very active in our church together. Then suddenly one day, totally unexpectedly, he walked out of my life and left me devastated! There was no infidelity involved. No one knows why, except our dear Lord and Savior, who to this day has not yet revealed to me the answer in spite of the many times I have cried out for an explanation.

However, out of this horrible experience of devastating rejection the Lord has given me a new life and I am truly happier than I have been in many years. My ex-husband has since remarried and he seems happy. But our precious daughter, who was a teenager when her father left, has bitterness and resentment still lingering inside of her, and she has never been able to forgive her father for leaving.

To this day she rarely talks to or visits her father, and it breaks my heart. I want so much for her and her father to love each other and have a father-daughter companionship that is so vital in this world today. I have suffered with my daughter and continually pray for her healing. She seems lost, unable to gain an identity.

Another woman wrote,

A most beautiful thing happened during the workshop yesterday. It has been extremely hard for me to forgive my ex-husband, not only because of what he did to me, but because of what he has done to our daughter. I have wrestled with this debtor a long time and had not realized how much resentment I was harboring. Yesterday I was able to forgive him, even though I didn't feel like it. Praise the Lord! I am free at last.

Now I wonder, could my lack of forgiveness have been holding back my daughter from making that choice to forgive her father? Oh, how I pray that the release that has come in my own spirit will spill over and she, too, will know the freedom that comes from forgiving her debtor.

Choose to forgive your ex-wife, your ex-husband.

Parents and Children

Children owe their parents honor, respect, and love. Instead some children have returned dishonor, disrespect, and rebellion. The parents feel the children owe them something different. They say, "After all I've done for you, and you don't appreciate me any more than this?" Are you withholding unconditional love from your children because of a debt you're expecting them pay to you? Do you need to forgive your children for

>   marrying the wrong person, one you didn't approve of?
>   behavior that is not morally right nor pleasing to you?
>   causing you pain by rebellion and waywardness?
>   not bringing you the honor you had hoped and prayed for?
>   being the prodigal, defiant, or gay?
>   demanding more than usual care from you?
>   coming at the wrong time?
>   having health problems or learning difficulties?

Parents, choose to forgive your children.

Children also must forgive their parents. God has made parents debtors to their children. It is not just something children expect; it is something they need. God has given parents this responsibility and they owe their children unconditional love. Instead, some parents have hurt, abused, demeaned, and made fun of the child, ignoring his or her needs and rights as a person. As a result, the child suffers hurt and tends to become resentful. Legitimate God-given needs have not been met. Many times this hurt and resentment is carried into adulthood. What a burden it becomes to the one who is carrying it!

Children, forgive your parents! The choice is yours. You can continue to carry the burden, or you can choose to be free from it by canceling the debt and giving up the resentment.

Some of us haven't admitted, even to ourselves, that we feel we have been wronged. To help identify the hurt, think about what bothers you about your parents, now or when you were growing up. Did one or both of your parents

demand perfection, making you feel you couldn't measure up?

desert the family?

use you to fulfill their unfulfilled dreams—educational, social, musical, athletic?

abuse you?

show favoritism: "Why can't you be like . . . ?"

wish you were the opposite sex?

not respect you as a person with needs?

not give you time, love, and proper training?

not release you to your own independence?

never admit they were wrong?

Some of you had parents who did fail you. Some of you were forsaken by parents, made to feel abandoned, put in foster homes, neglected, ignored, or adopted out. Some of you were badly abused. Perhaps you feel your parents should have given you a better upbringing, a more honorable home, a better church life, a finer education, or a more adequate chance in society.

Will you forgive your debtor parents, even without understanding why they gave you up, why they beat you, why they treated you wrongly, or why they divorced? Forgiveness is a choice. Choose to forgive your parents.

Friends and Christian Leaders

Friendships of every kind are subject to the same abuses as any other close relationship. Has a so-called friend ever

> betrayed your friendship?
> rejected you?
> seemed to use you for a time, then when she or he became interested in someone or something else, ignored your friendship commitment?
> date raped you or led you into sexual involvement?

Choose to forgive your insensitive friend.

Christian leaders, both para-church and church, owe us the example of the kind of life they talk about. We think, *They owed me a consistent Christian life and they didn't pay.* They've fallen and we've been disillusioned. Choose to forgive them for

> how they treated you.
> not preaching sermons that met your needs.
> being uncaring, cold, and unfeeling.

In-laws

What bugs you about your daughter- or son-in-law?

- He or she is not good enough for our son or daughter.
- He or she doesn't do things our way.
- He or she isn't treating our grandchildren right.
- He or she is too . . .

What bugs you about your own in-laws?

- They're too possessive of their son or daughter.
- They're always interfering in our lives.
- They don't like how we spend our money.
- They criticize how we handle the children.
- They're never pleased with . . .
- They always try to tell us how to . . .
- They always expect us to . . .

A Christian woman confided her own struggles with her in-laws.

For almost thirty years I harbored a strong dislike, if not hate, for my mother-in-law. I felt very justified in feeling that way because she has always been a strong-willed, domineering person. She had often tried to interfere with and influence decisions that we as a couple needed to make. Each time she was with us, I added grievances to my already lengthy list against her.

Then, for the first time, I attended the workshop. I heard so many wonderful truths that helped and encouraged me. I also realized that the Lord was tenderly but definitely putting his finger on this matter of my bad relationship with my husband's mother. I felt convicted about it. I knew that I lacked love for her, regardless of her attitude toward me. But I resisted admitting my guilt. It was, after all, her fault! She was my debtor.

Finally, I surrendered all my terrible feelings to the Lord and asked him to help me make things right with my mother-in-law. I knew I would have to give up my resentment toward her and to ask her to forgive me for my lack of love for her all those years. Only the Lord could give me such grace!

It was a whole year before I was able to carry through my commitment to the Lord in this matter. The time came for us to visit her in a distant city. I was now very eager, in a nervous sort of way, to talk with her. I looked for the earliest opportunity when we might talk alone. It finally came on our last day with her.

I sat in her kitchen, willing to speak to her, but the words just wouldn't come out! I could not believe it. I prayed and just forced the words out. "Mom, I know that our relationship over the years has been poor. I have not shown love to you as I ought, and I ask your forgiveness for my lack of love."

She reacted minimally, but that did not matter to me. What was exciting to me was losing all the bad feelings I had nurtured over the years. They were gone and have never returned. I didn't expect that! The debt she owed me was canceled. And what a relief to be rid of such a heavy burden!

Consider the price of an unforgiving spirit. It builds up hostility, resentment, and bitterness. It can result in physical weakness and disease, and can cause much pain and suffering personally and in relationships. An unforgiving spirit hinders our sense of peace and contentment, our power from the Lord to cope with the events of our lives, the support our friends would like to give us, and the building of a positive self-image.

We must forgive our debtors, for our own sake, as well as for their sake and for God's sake and glory. However, it is important to remember that what any of these debtors have done may not be excusable, but it is forgivable.

Yourself

One person that I met bemoaned, "The hardest part is to forgive myself!" It may well be the hardest thing to do. You have been holding yourself debtor to yourself. You feel you owed yourself a better reputation, more purity, the honor of having more sense, and more stability.

A bride of three months tells how she was finally able to forgive herself.

My boyfriend and I talked about marriage less than a month after we met. You might say it was love at first sight. We dated several months and are now happily married. My problem? We're expecting our first baby in October—five months after the wedding.

I've asked the Lord for forgiveness, but I cannot understand how he could forgive such a thing. I was raised in a Christian home. My father is a minister. I felt that I was a black sheep, a disgrace to the family, and couldn't forgive myself for what had happened.

I received letters of love and acceptance from all my brothers and sisters and my parents. Their overwhelming unconditional love helped me to finally receive God's unconditional love and forgiveness. And at the workshop today I have once and for all forgiven myself. Thank you, Verna, you've opened a door of peace for me—one I had shut on myself.

As a daughter, do you feel you have failed your family? As a spouse, do you feel you have failed your partner? Forgive yourself. As a parent, do you feel you have failed your child? As a widow or widower, do you feel you didn't do all you should have for your partner before death? As a person, do you feel you were a failure as a friend—in Christian witness, in the sexual area, in compassion? Forgive yourself.

As a person who was sexually molested as a child, do you have a small voice that haunts you, saying, "You should have known better; shame on you." Give up the shame, the self-condemnation. Forgive yourself.

As a divorced person, forgive yourself for the mistakes you made in the relationship. Forgive yourself for the things you wish you hadn't done. Forgive yourself for the divorce itself. Be free from the guilt and give up the shame.

The only way you will ever be able to forgive yourself is by first receiving God's forgiveness. Much of the misery and unrest we experience today is because we feel contempt, disgust, and shame for sins and failures of the past. We are letting the enemy of our souls and our own self-accusing spirit continually harass and shame us for the sins and failures of the past. We feel terribly guilty when all the while God is waiting to forgive. Actually he has already forgiven, but for that forgiveness to be effective in life, one needs to enter into the reality of it through choosing to believe that Jesus Christ has done what he said he would.

A long time ago God sent his Son to die on the cross to pay the full price for all your sins and failures. He has already paid the debt you owed, a debt that you could never pay, even if you spent an eternity shaming yourself or feeling guilty about it.

Scripture says he is "ready to forgive" (Ps. 86:5). Ready to forgive! He has blotted out our sins, removing them from us as far as the east is from the west (see Ps. 103:12 and Isa. 44:22). Honor him by believing what he says about *all* sin, which includes your sin. Instead of being suspicious about whether or not he is telling you the truth or whether it applies to your specific sins, believe him. Accept the fact that you're forgiven and that he has freed you from guilt.

Then, deliberately choose to forgive yourself! Don't keep shaming yourself, calling yourself a failure, or digging up the past looking for more things you should or shouldn't have done. This reviewing of the past and the failure to believe in God's forgiveness is at the heart of most of our struggles to forgive ourselves. Decide to forgive yourself. It's a choice you must make.

A young mother testified,

Two very heavy burdens have been lifted from my heart today. First, my children are no longer a burden to me, but a joy. It has been my way to become extremely upset with my two small children—to the point where I would look to God and scream, "Lord, I can't take it any more!" And in my inner self I felt I could only find relief from this if God would take my children from me. Then, how guilty I felt for thinking such thoughts. Through the workshop today I realized what precious gifts my children are. I wanted to stand up in the audience and shout!

The second burden was the guilt that haunted me. Until now, I hadn't realized that, although I knew God had forgiven me, I had never forgiven myself for those wrong thoughts about my children. The guilt has been so tremendous, I cry every time I remember. Now I cry for joy because that awful, heavy weight of guilt has been lifted.

Say repeatedly to yourself: "I am forgiven! Jesus Christ has paid the full price for all my sin. God has forgiven me, and I now choose to forgive myself. I'm trusting God to make that past wrong work for good in my life and in my ministry to others. I trust him to create beauty from ashes."

God's forgiving grace, operative in us, makes it possible for us to forgive others. Before we check out some simple helps toward a forgiving heart, there's one other person we must consider as we answer the question, Who are my debtors?

20

Is God
My Debtor?

Many times we get angry at God for allowing things to happen to us that we think should never have happened. We rationalize that he owes us a better personality or more favorable circumstances. He really should not have allowed

the temperament and personality and struggles I've been stuck with.

my spouse to divorce me after I believed he would save our marriage.

my child, spouse, friend, or parent to become sick, to become an invalid, to have an accident, or to die.

the one I love—child, spouse, parent, friend—to be so insensitive or ruthless.

these awful circumstances to happen—sexual abuse, imprisonment, financial distress, flood, earthquake, and so forth.

We may be asking, Why does God allow people who are living in sin to have better jobs, better health, nicer homes, and even well-behaved children, and I don't have these things, though I'm committed to him and have lived for him a long time?

Jan was a junior in college. Every so often she would come in, plop herself down in my chair, and express again how discouraged she was with life, with herself, and with her relationship to the Lord. She felt that she had failed him, and she was disappointed in herself and her inconsistencies.

Usually I just quietly listened as she expressed her discouragement and terrible sense of failure. After this had happened several times, I said to her, "Jan, is there anything in your life you wish had never happened? Something that has deeply hurt you?"

Slowly she began.

Well, when I was thirteen my mother died. I've always wondered why she died just when I needed her the most to be my companion, to teach me the things girls need to know. I feel I've missed so much in life, that I'm not all I could have been if I had had my mother with me to love me and guide me during those crucial years.

I just can't understand why God would allow a teenager to be without her mother during those very critical years. Why would God allow it to happen to me? Doesn't he care about me? Doesn't he love me as he loves other girls?

Jan was really saying, "God owed me a mother to guide me through my critical teenage years. Why didn't he pay his debt?"

Some people have prayed about things for a long time, yet nothing happens. Why doesn't God answer? A wife whose husband was not a Christian wrote,

For years I have been praying that my husband would become a Christian to complete the kind of home I would like to raise our family in. My prayers continue to be unanswered. I hadn't realized that I had been holding resentment against God and my husband because this was not happening as soon as I had been expecting. I kept asking the Lord, "Why?"

Thank you ever so much for being used of the Lord to bring my resentment to light. I pray the Lord will give me patience in prayer and the strength to wait until God fulfills his will, not mine! I have canceled the debt I thought God owed me. Glory has filled my soul.

What had she been saying? "God is my debtor. God owes me an answer to my prayer now! He owes me the salvation of my husband and the right kind of home in which to raise the children."

No More Evil Thoughts about God

Obviously God doesn't owe us a thing. But when I have been operating on the premise that he does owe me something and he isn't paying, then I need to acknowledge my hostility toward God—my inward demand for payment—and realize that I need to forgive God, my debtor, as this mother did.

We have four children; two are adopted. One of the adopted girls became a runaway at age thirteen and is now in Youth Authority at age sixteen. Her sister is also becoming rebellious at home and school. I realized today that I was beginning to feel resentment toward God for giving me these girls. After all, I reasoned, hadn't I taken these girls in and given them a good home? Didn't God owe me something—at least less trouble—for all my efforts?

This inner attitude of *I don't like it,* if expressed on the outside would be something like doubling our fist, shaking it at God, and saying, "Why? Why did you allow that? I don't like it!" One young couple shared how they overcame this attitude.

> *Last September we came into repossession of a condo that we had sold four years earlier. The buyer decided to walk out on the contract, owing us five thousand dollars. This was a great burden to us.*
>
> *Our immediate reaction was anger and frustration. We couldn't think about it without getting upset and depressed. Over and over we complained, "It's not fair!" After many months of such growling, we realized we were actually murmuring against God. We were holding him as our debtor. He owed us a better deal. Why had he let the buyer default?*
>
> *When we finally came to accept the whole thing as from God—allowed by him, and in his providential care—the bitterness, the anxiety, and the depression over the financial burden lifted. The circumstance has not changed, but we daily choose to believe that God himself, and what he chooses to provide at this moment, is all we need.*

Do you have a fist clenched in God's face? Are you inwardly thinking, *I've served him faithfully all these years and what do I have in return?* Or *I read my Bible and pray as I ought, why doesn't he bless me?* With these thoughts and attitudes we're really thinking that God is our debtor. He owes us a better deal in life than this. Colossians 3:8 from the Phillips version says it so graphically; we are to have "no more evil thoughts or words about God."

There's Liberty in Release

This triumphant letter gives powerful testimony to the liberty enjoyed by one who does not hold God debtor for the bad circumstances and events of life.

My twenty-two-year-old son was killed in an auto accident four years ago. When the state troopers left my home after telling me the news, I immediately claimed Romans 8:28 and asked God to be glorified somehow through this.

The confidence and assurance I had was truly supernatural. Thank God I had already released my children to him, so there was no blame in my heart at all. I knew they belonged to him and that he controlled their lives. God carried me so lovingly during that hard time; so much so that I even felt praise in my heart at the funeral. God is so good.

To experience the contentment and peace of God and thus be free to reach out in ministry to others we must not hold God as our debtor.

21

How to Forgive My Debtors

When we talk about forgiving our debtors, we're talking about real debts and real debtors—those who owe us something and haven't paid; those who have hurt us deeply, usually by violating our rights or failing to meet our needs. They wronged us! What they have done is not excusable, but it is forgivable. We can forgive them if we choose to do so. You may be thinking, *How can I do that when I have been hurt so deeply?* If your heart's desire is to forgive, but you find it humanly impossible to cancel the debt, to give up the resentment that may have been lodging there over many years, let these simple helps lead you on in your pilgrimage toward forgiveness. Sometimes forgiving your debtor is a process.

Recognize Hurt and Resentment

You need to recognize that you hurt and that you hurt because someone has treated you wrongly. He or she may or may not have intended hurt; that is not the issue.

The issue is that you feel the hurt deeply because you feel you have been treated unfairly.

You suffered pain when you did not deserve it or when it was not necessary. You feel pain because the other person owed you respect, acceptance, faithfulness, and confidence. Instead the person gave insult, rejection, and betrayal of trust.

You need to recognize that your hurt has issued into resentment. You do not wish your offender well. You may even secretly wish him ill, wanting to see him suffer because he has made you suffer. You have the inner attitude, *He should pay me what he owes.* The very least that you expect is an acknowledgement of the mistake or wrong and an apology. In your spirit you demand payment.

You need to let your body talk to you in this regard. Headaches, chest pains, and stomach problems have often been traced back to feelings of anxiety, guilt, and resentment. Is your body giving you any such warnings as it did for this lady?

In 1978, the Enriched Living Workshop came to Omaha. I had suffered for nine months previous to that time with miserable gastritis. I missed the first day because of a drug dimout—the antispasmodics spaced me out. The second day I came only in the morning and all I remember hearing Verna say was, "My doctor said that many stomach problems are caused by suppressed anger and resentment." When I went home, I sat in my prayer chair. "Oh, Lord, if that's it, show me."

My mother had put herself into the hospital with prescription drug abuse and had come near to death. What was worse, she had never accepted responsibility for what she had done. It took me an hour or two to be able to let go of my right to sit in judgment and to forgive her, but by God's grace I did come to that place.

Within a week the major symptoms of my gastritis were gone. It took a few more months before the damage to my digestion was more or less healed. It may never be completely healed, but it doesn't cause me any more major difficulty. We really can mess ourselves up with bitterness and judgmentalism.

Choose Forgiveness

You must choose to forgive your debtor. Forgiveness is a decision. You need to change your attitude of vengeance to an attitude of canceling the debt. Your making a deliberate choice to cancel the debt and give up your resentment against the other—that's forgiveness.

You must forgive on the basis of your own full and free forgiveness in Christ. It's only fair. How do you feel toward the man in Matthew 18 who wouldn't forgive his own debtor when his own much, much larger debt was fully forgiven?

You must forgive on the basis of having all the will of God in your life. God commands it for your good. You are to be obedient.

You must forgive on the basis of your own need for emotional, physical, and spiritual health. For future health you need all channels clear to God for an awareness of his forgiveness, his love, his compassion, and his strength.

Mary Ellen wrote to me about her difficulty with forgiveness.

When I was a child, my father seemed totally insensitive to me and my feelings. Sometimes he would make fun of me and laugh at me when I wet my pants or wet the bed. I got angry at him for the way he tried to make me quit sucking my thumb. After he put medicine on my thumb,

*he'd grab my hands and force my thumb into my mouth.
He knew I hated it and would laugh at my defeat and his
victory!*

*Why should I forgive my dad? He was wrong. I guess I'm
resentful because he's never been sorry. What I really want is
for my dad to look at his past, see some of his mistakes, and
say, "Mary Ellen, I was wrong. I wasn't sensitive to you. I didn't
express my love to you or take responsibilities in certain areas."
That's what I desire, but it doesn't happen. How do you deal
with forgiveness when the other person isn't remorseful?*

Mary Ellen finds it impossible to forgive her dad
because she's holding him debtor. True, he was wrong!
The Bible clearly says, "Fathers, do not provoke your
children, lest they become discouraged" (Col. 3:21).
Mary Ellen's father owed his child love, understanding,
and sensitivity instead of ridicule, shame, and a power
struggle. He owed her respect as a person with needs.
Instead he treated her as an object to be humiliated,
laughed at, and made fun of. He truly is a debtor to her.
What he did was inexcusable. We don't excuse him or
minimize the hurt, but Mary Ellen needs to forgive her
dad to be free within herself as well as to possibly open
a door to build a relationship with him.

Forgiveness is a choice. Mary Ellen has a choice to
make. She can continue to hold her father debtor and
demand payment in her spirit, or she can choose to forgive him, and free him from the debt by canceling it.
There will be no true release in her own spirit until she
does.

One person angrily retorted, "Do you mean to imply
I have to forgive my offender before he asks my forgiveness?" For your own sake you must, even if he never
acknowledges his wrong or asks for your forgiveness.
It's your unforgiving spirit that will damage you the
most. For your own sake, choose to forgive your debtor.

Put Forgiveness into Action

Accept the pain of the hurts. Be willing to bear suffering. "Father, you've forgiven me. I choose to forgive. Fill me with your love that forgives. I trust you for grace sufficient to forgive just as Christ has forgiven me. I am willing to suffer that the other one might be healed."

Inwardly release the person from all debts, canceling the debts and giving up the resentments against the other. Give the hurts, the hurter, and all related problems over to the Lord Jesus. Trust him to do what is best for the one who hurt you as well as for yourself. Trust him to turn those hurts into benefits in your own life and in your ministry to others now and in the future.

Many find that one helpful way of handing the hurts over to God is to thank God in respect to the situation. Thank him not necessarily for the painful event, but for the promise that he will work all things together for good. Thanking God can not only be a way of expressing your confident trust in him in spite of the circumstances but also a channel for releasing the person from your unforgiving spirit.

A young woman from Georgia wrote,

For six years I've had a chronic illness. Although it is treatable, I have had to change my educational and career plans in order to adjust to the physical limitations it has put on me. I have been resentful toward God for my affliction, but today at the workshop I was finally able to thank God for my weakness and tell him that I trust him for the outcome. This is a big relief. Now Psalm 119:71 is mine.

Another, from Ohio, experienced that same release.

Recently I was hurt very badly. Even though I forgave the person, I didn't feel good about him. Today at the workshop I thanked

*God for both the person and the difficult circumstance that his
actions brought into our lives. Something wonderful happened,
a minor miracle. For the first time I'm excited to see the person,
to throw my arms around him in love, and to see what good thing
God will bring from all this. At last I am free, all because I
expressed my trust in God by thanking him.*

Allow God to change your attitude toward the other
person by focusing on how you can minister to the person's needs, weaknesses, limitations, and hurts instead
of focusing on what he or she owes you. Concentrate on
letting God change the resentful, revengeful spirit that
wishes the person ill into a loving, serving attitude—ministering to the person's needs and wishing him or her well.

Pray for the well-being of the one who hurt you.
Matthew 5:44 says, "But I say to you, love your enemies,
and pray for those who persecute you" (NASB). Ask yourself if you need to apologize or make restitution for any
ways you may have wronged, hurt, or sinned against the
person. Determine to do just that.

Don't expect to continually *feel* forgiveness. If you do
not feel forgiveness, continue to take your stand on the
facts and declare, "I have forgiven and I continue to forgive." If a repeated hurt occurs, declare, "I forgive again.
I forgive my debtor."

Pray that God will completely heal your emotional
hurts so that even the memories of the event will no
longer be painful. The process for healing the hurt and
the memory of the pain will now begin. When the wound
is cleansed from all bitterness through forgiveness, real
healing begins.

Plan Restoration

Pray about any further responsibility you may have
toward the other person in restoring the relationship.

Full restoration and reconciliation require the cooperation of both the offender and the offended, and may or may not take place—depending on the willingness of both parties involved. Your own healing begins with forgiveness and can take place whether or not there is total restoration in the relationship. Forgiveness depends on only one person—you. But restoration depends on two people, so you can't take total responsibility for that. Only do your part.

The choice is not to try to erase the past, ignore it, or pretend it didn't happen. The debt is a real debt, and as far as your attitude toward it is concerned, it must either be paid by your debtor or be officially canceled by you. When you forgive, you cancel the debt and you give up the resentment against the person. Will you write "canceled" across all those claim checks? Will you choose to forgive your debtors? That is, will you give up your resentment and cancel the debt? Will you give to God your expectations of the person and release him or her from the pressure of your expectations and your resentment?

John Henry Jowett writes about forgiveness.

> True forgiveness is a very strong and clean virtue. There is a counterfeit forgiveness which is unworthy of the name. It is full of "buts" and "ifs" and "maybes." It moves with reluctance, it takes back with one hand what it gives with the other. It forgives, but it cannot forget. It forgives, but it can never trust again. It forgives, but things can never be the same as they were.[11]

You must make the choice. If, in your spirit, you demand payment and maintain an unforgiving spirit, it will inevitably add an overload of stress and take its toll in your emotional, spiritual, and physical well-being. If, instead, you choose to forgive your debtor, you will be free and at peace with God, yourself, and others. As far as your responsibility goes, you will greatly diminish stress in your life.

22

How to Rise Above Past Failures and Sins

Forgiving your debtors—God, others, yourself—is a prerequisite to rising above past failures and sins. When you do this, resentment exerts no more power over you. Giving up resentment toward God gives you new closeness to him, new confidence in his power, and opens the channels of your life for the flow of his all-sufficient grace. Giving up resentment toward others gives you new courage, freedom, and power to cope with the situation. Giving up self-blame, shame, and feelings of guilt will give you a much greater ability to manage the stress that your sin or failure has caused.

These additional suggestions will also give release if considered seriously and put into practice.

Face your failure or sin realistically. Deal definitely, decisively, and appropriately with it. If it is sin, name the sin, and repent of it. Confess it to the Lord and, if it is necessary and appropriate, confess it to the person involved. Wherein there is failure and that failure has touched other people, admit it to them. It will be freeing to you if you admit it and apologize rather than try to hide or forget it.

Commit your failure and yourself to the Lord. Trust the Lord to use that failure or mistake for his glory. Ask and trust him to so overrule in regard to your sin that he will use it for your growth and ministry and for his glory. Ask him to teach you the lessons you need to learn from that failure or sin. Thank God that he can use that failure and thank him for his instruction to you through it. Someone has spoken of the gift of failure, explaining that God sometimes lets us fail in order to teach us significant lessons and to bless us more abundantly.

Receive God's forgiveness. Choose to believe that God has forgiven you just as he said he would: "If we confess our sins, He is faithful and just to forgive us our sins and to cleanse us from all unrighteousness" (1 John 1:9). If we confess, he forgives. Believe him! Thank him that you are forgiven for that sin. Thank him that you are free from the guilt of that sin. By faith receive his full forgiveness and cleansing from all unrighteousness.

Forgive yourself. Now, based on God's forgiveness of you, deliberately choose to forgive yourself and not accuse or demean or shame yourself any longer. Take on the mind-set of the apostle Paul, "Forgetting those things which are behind and reaching forward to those things which are ahead" (Phil. 3:13).

Paul surely had some things in his past to regret or to feel guilty about, but based on God's redeeming love and forgiving grace, he chose to believe he was forgiven. He would not let the enemy harass him with guilt over the remembrance of those things any more. His only memory of his past was to let it serve as a reminder of God's great forgiving, overruling grace (see 1 Tim. 1:12–17). You, too, must decide not to give in to guilt.

Keep a watch on your self-talk, your inner conversations. Correct the lies. Take your stand on the truth, as we shared in chapter 14. It's the truth that shall make and keep you free (see John 8:32). Do not tolerate such lies or such self-reproach as, "God surely can't forgive me for this. People will never forgive me, and I can never forgive myself. I never should have . . . If only I would have . . . instead." Choose to believe that God's power is adequate and that his grace is sufficient to cause all things to work together for good. Let your self-talk be of thanksgiving and trustful confidence in God rather than self-reproach, accusation, and shame.

Choose to trust God's overruling grace. Expect God to use this failure or sin for good in your life—for growth and learning, as a stepping-stone, a growth step, perhaps to humble you and cause you to see how much you need to depend on him. Ask and expect him to use it in your life to enhance your ministry to others, to help you to

> be more understanding, forgiving, tolerant, and sensitive of others.
> be more supportive, loving, gentle, and kind.
> share what God did for you and how he can help them in a like need.
> pray for others instead of criticizing them.

Have realistic self-expectations. Be fair in what you expect of yourself, especially when it comes to failure. Are you reasonable in your expectations of your performance, or do you have totally unrealistic perfectionistic standards that you cannot possibly reach? If so, learn to be realistic; don't expect perfection.

Trust God to give you victory over sin. Trust God to make his resurrection power operative in you and to give you victory over sin. That power can enable you to withstand the temptation to sin again. We can claim his promise to make us more than conquerors, and to work in us both to will and to do of his good pleasure. We can choose to die to sin and live by his resurrection power, yielding our members as instruments of righteousness unto God and not yielding unto sin (see Rom. 6:4, 12–19; 8:37; Phil. 2:13).

Here again we must choose and refuse in cooperation with him. In this way we will be assuming proper responsibility. As Romans 6:12, 14 challenges, "Do not let sin reign in your mortal body that you should obey its lusts. . . . For sin shall not be master over you" (NASB).

Barbara shared with me her difficulty in accepting God's forgiveness.

Thank you, Verna, for the workshop I attended last month in Dallas. I only wish I could have had it when my children were growing up. I'm a mother of four and a grandmother of six. I was a very stern mother and really never had any help with authority from their father. Our children still feel this, although my two daughters who have children understand more and more.

I brought my youngest daughter, mother of three, along to this workshop. She has been enjoying it and has already been applying it. I pray for them every day that their child-raising years will be more joyful than mine. Verna, don't misunderstand—I loved them. We did have many fun times, but I feel guilty for my overharshness. I still ask God at times to forgive me for wrongdoing. Is this OK?

Why does this woman still feel guilty for her overharshness, her sternness? What should she do to rise above this past failure? Let's check the steps we outlined above.

She has already faced her failure. We don't know if she has acknowledged this to her children and asked their forgiveness. If not, she needs to do that.

She needs to commit that failure and herself to the Lord and trust the Lord to use that failure for his glory. She needs to ask and trust him to overrule the pain and hurt that the children experienced.

She needs not only to ask God's forgiveness, which she has done many, many times, but she needs to believe in and receive his forgiveness.

She needs to forgive herself—not letting the remembrance of her failure condemn her but motivate her to love and to good works. This she is doing. She brought her daughter to the workshop to learn how to be a better parent. She is praying for her children every day that they will be guided in raising their children.

She needs to keep a watch on her self-talk as indicated by her comment, "I still ask God at times to forgive me for wrongdoing." Her current self-talk is continual self-reproach and questioning of God's forgiveness. This needs to be changed into a God-talk of thanksgiving for his forgiveness and a restful confidence in him.

She needs to choose to trust God's overruling grace for her own life and for the outcome of her actions in the lives of her children.

She needs to be fair in her expectations of herself as a parent. Parents are human. Parents will make mistakes. All God asks of her is that she be open to learn and grow and always be willing to take the necessary steps to correct her failure or sin insofar as she can.

Forgiveness is giving up your right to be resentful against another or to hurt the one who has hurt you. It is canceling the debt of another. But forgiveness is not meant to perpetuate an attitude of domination by one person over another. Nor is it intended to destroy your ability to be yourself or your right to stand up for yourself.

Living the forgiving lifestyle does not mean that we become doormats and let everyone trample over us. If we allowed this, we would not be taking responsibility to maintain our rights for our own good, for the good of the other person, and for the good of the relationship—all for the glory of God and to fulfill his purposes.

It is not right for us to make it easy for others to abuse us. If we do, we make it difficult for them to respect us and we encourage their wrong behavior.

Forgiveness rises out of strength, not weakness. It is a choice that demands courage. It springs from a heart that has chosen personal-circle fullness in the person of God himself.

PART 4

MISBELIEF #2:

I MUST LOOK OUT FOR NUMBER ONE

23

MINISTER
TO OTHERS

A disgruntled wife told how the evening often began at their house.

When my husband was late, I'd greet him at the door, or even go out into the yard and say, "Well, where have you been? Why didn't you call, or at least leave me a note telling me you were going out?" I went on like this all the way into the house.

While fixing dinner for him, I wouldn't say a word. I enjoyed slamming doors and pots and pans. I really did it up good. I sat at the table with him, but I would not eat! "How could I be hungry," I'd whine, "when I was worried sick about you? It spoiled my appetite!"

Hateful? Maybe, but I had to watch out for myself, didn't I? My husband was certainly not interested in my happiness or convenience!

In response to a very typical daily occurrence, this wife was expressing one of our most insidious misbeliefs as seen in figure 23.1.

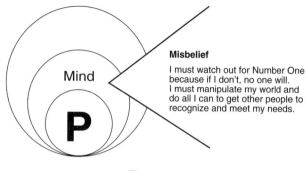

Figure 23.1

The first mention of this wrong belief is in the very first chapters of the very first book of the Bible. God had filled Adam's personal circle (see figure 23.2) with himself and many added blessings.

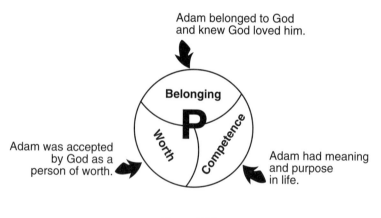

Figure 23.2

At any given moment it is possible to have personal-circle fullness with God himself filling our circle. However, his perfect plan is to also give us the added joy of people who minister to us in these three areas of need.

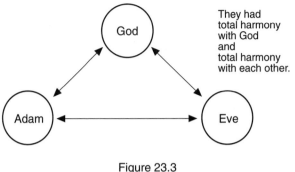

Figure 23.3

Therefore, to Adam, God gave Eve. So here were Adam and Eve. Each enjoyed personal-circle fullness in God (see figure 23.3). Each was ministering to the needs of the other. They enjoyed and appreciated the things God chose to provide for them moment by moment. They were not self-centered or out to get what they could for themselves. Rather, they were out to give to one another, to minister to the other person's needs.

In Genesis 3 we read how sin entered the world and absolutely shattered this perfect harmony (see figure 23.4). Instead of other-centeredness there was

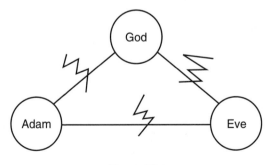

Figure 23.4

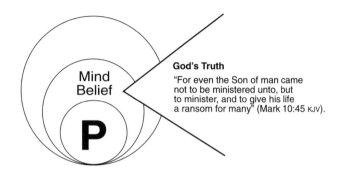

Figure 23.5

self-centeredness. This was the origin of the misbelief: I must watch out for Number One, because if I don't, no one else will. This dangerous, peace-destroying, stress-producing misbelief must be countered with the truth of God (see figure 23.5).

Mark 10:45 speaks of the Lord Jesus who gave his life to pay the penalty for our sins that we might become children of God by faith in the completed work of Christ on the cross. It also speaks of Jesus' whole life attitude, which was to minister to others.

Never Operate from a Deficit

This should also be the great passion of our lives—to minister unto others. But the only way we can freely minister is to know personal-circle fullness in our own lives, and to have all the channels clear—holding no one as our debtor. It has been said that Christians should never operate from a deficit but from fullness and forgiveness.

This became painfully real to me one Saturday as I stood in the supermarket line with ten people ahead of me. Many of the carts were overflowing with a week's supply of groceries. My day was full and busy and the last thing I wanted was to wait in a long, slow line to purchase a few items. It was also becoming obvious that the first lady in my line was having a problem and slowing progress even more. She was frustrated and embarrassed and alone. But the group of strangers in the line suddenly experienced a mysterious, silent drawing together. After all, weren't we all suffering together? We sighed with impatience. We rolled our eyes at one another, obviously disgusted with the first lady in line. We made sure she knew we considered her a menace to Saturday supermarket shoppers—especially us!

In less time than any of our so-called group would care to admit, the problem was solved, we sailed through the checkout, and waltzed through the automatic doors. Somehow, though, the satisfaction of our mutual impatience evaporated as we walked out with our brown bags.

Here I had a lovely opportunity to minister to the needs of many people, especially to the frustrated one at the front of the line, but instead I chose the selfish route. I was even drawing attention to myself and encouraging angry feelings in others, silently manipulating them to join in my impatience, putting the first lady in line in an even more embarrassing situation.

When I act like that, I am obviously not ministering to the needs of others. I am expecting to be ministered to by trying to manipulate the people and events in my world to recognize and meet my needs. I am actually saying that God and what he chose to provide at that moment in the supermarket were not enough to fill my personal circle.

God wants to come to the other person through me. What an opportunity I had missed to let his patience, his kindness, and his forgiveness minister to that line of people at the checkout counter!

God's Chosen Grace Carriers

We are God's chosen representatives to carry his grace to others. We can minister that grace by giving cups of cold water. We can minister that grace by pouring love into other people's love cups.

If I have found love and worthwhileness in Christ, I can come to another person with personal-circle fullness. If I have chosen personal-circle fullness, then I don't need to have another person behave in such a way that will affirm my personal-circle needs and make me feel like a significant person. It is a fact: I am already significant in Christ.

For example, a mother who has found completeness in Christ doesn't have to have her child behave in an acceptable way so that people will think she is a good mother. Her motive in discipline is the good of the child and the honor of God. This frees her to minister to the needs of the child, whether or not she is understood by other people.

Remember, God our Creator planned for us to go out in loving ministry, giving to others and affirming others in their triad of personal needs. I can unselfishly minister to you because I am a whole person, complete in Christ. My basic, personal needs to be loved and feel worthwhile are ultimately met in God and what he chooses to provide. I am secure in God's unconditional, unfailing, everlasting love. My life has value. I'm a person of worth. Because I know this personal-circle fullness, I can be his personal agent to carry his grace to others.

Laura expressed it this way.

God is showing me how tender, loving, gentle, and compassionate he is through other people. I did not learn this through my own father and mother. My father left us when I was two and my mother always claimed it was because of my sister and me that he left.

My mother refused to assume any responsibility for the marriage breakup, so she blamed us. As a result I didn't have a good image of my earthly father and mother, nor of my heavenly Father. But now I am becoming aware of God's tender love for me as he is expressing himself in loving ways through the actions of others.

What a privilege we have of being God's hand-picked representatives and carriers of his grace! Let's find out who needs that grace and how we can minister it to those in need.

24

ROBBERS
OF PERSONAL DIGNITY
AND WORTH

A wife was bemoaning to me the bad attitude she had had as she came home from work one day very tired.

My husband is in the process of changing jobs and he was full of things to tell me about his new job. Instead of listening with interest, I blurted out, "Honey, I'm very tired. Just let me unwind!" I'm sure you don't have to think too hard to know what the tone of my voice was while saying this.

Perhaps you can also guess the results. He got very angry and said he was never going to talk to me about anything anymore! Of course I was very sorry the minute the words were out of my mouth, but the damage was done. I had put a terrible damper on his spirit by not being interested in the exciting things he had to tell me at that moment.

By a few simple, little words said at the wrong time and in the wrong manner, I blew my whole opportunity to minister to the needs of my husband. Instead, I was letting this ever-present misbelief, that I should look out for Number One, control my thinking. I was doing a fantastic job of watching out for me!

Jesus left us his example of "ministering unto," but he also had something to say about this in his teaching. It came in story form as he answered a question put to him by a certain lawyer (see Luke 10:25–37 NASB).

And behold, a certain lawyer stood up and put Him [Jesus] to the test, saying, "Teacher, what shall I do to inherit eternal life?"

And He said to him, "What is written in the Law? How does it read to you?"

And he answered and said, "You shall love the LORD your God with all your heart, and with all your soul, and with all your strength, and with all your mind; and your neighbor as yourself."

And He said to him, "You have answered correctly; do this, and you will live."

But wishing to justify himself, he said to Jesus, "And who is my neighbor?"

Jesus replied and said, "A certain man was going down from Jerusalem to Jericho; and he fell among robbers, and they stripped him and beat him, and went off leaving him half dead.

"And by chance a certain priest was going down on that road, and when he saw him, he passed by on the other side.

"And likewise a Levite also, when he came to the place and saw him, passed by on the other side.

"But a certain Samaritan, who was on a journey, came upon him; and when he saw him, he felt compassion, and came to him, and bandaged up his wounds, pouring oil and wine on them; and he put him on his own beast, and brought him to an inn, and took care of him.

"And on the next day he took out two denarii and gave them to the innkeeper and said, 'Take care of him; and whatever more you spend, when I return, I will repay you.'

"Which of these three do you think proved to be a neighbor to the man who fell into the robbers' hands?"

And he said, "The one who showed mercy toward him." And Jesus said to him, "Go and do the same."

Someone in your path has fallen among robbers. He has been stripped, wounded, and left half-dead—with his cup for love bone dry. Life doesn't seem worth living. The robbers can be many kinds of things.

Perhaps he had parents, or other significant figures, who were too busy to give him needed attention. Perhaps he had parents whose own love cups were too dry for them to notice his needs or give to those needs. Perhaps he had parents who were too wrapped up in self-realization and personal achievement and had no time to think of him. He might have been a latchkey child.

His parents may have been bothered and frustrated because of his conception. His parents may have been resentful and rejecting of his sex or another aspect of his person at birth. Did they fail to meet his triad of personal-circle needs so he never had the confidence of belonging, counting, and being capable?

Was he treated as an object rather than a person? Was physical or sexual abuse a regular part of his home life?

Perhaps the important people in his life verbally lashed out at him, wrongly accusing him with anger and impatience. Perhaps because of death or divorce he felt rejected by them. They might have been overprotective, afraid to let him grow up and become his own person.

Was his father an angry man? Was his mother an authoritarian? Did they cling to him for their own security and thus stifle his freedom to develop in a healthy way?

All of this has contributed to the person he is today. He is a wounded person. He has been robbed of so much, and he probably has habits and traits that make many want to pass by on the other side.

We excuse ourselves with: "He isn't my type," or "I'm just not drawn to him." We point out: "He's obnoxious and proud"; "he talks too much"; "he talks too little." We complain: "He's too shy"; "he's too aggressive"; "he's stupid"; "he's too smart."

Perhaps the most realistic of all is when we honestly confess, "I'm afraid of what people will think of me when they see me with him."

We can be like the priest and Levite and pay no attention or turn away from a wounded person. Or, we can let God use us to be an agent of his love, his mercy, and his compassion for the wounded and the thirsty.

As we each become more and more secure in God's love and experience personal-circle fullness in more and more situations, we are more and more able to become pitchers—pouring love into the outstretched cups all around us.

25

Biblical Guidelines for Ministering to Others

One lady in a workshop said, "Verna, we don't know how. Please teach us how to love others." That's a pretty big order, but I am going to speak as specifically and practically as I can, as we seek to discover how to really show love to one another.

My friend, Jan, related her own Good Samaritan story.

Our sixteen-year-old son recently had an accident on his ten-speed bike. After an oral surgeon sewed up his mouth and another surgeon stitched his nose, he had to go back into surgery to have the inside of his broken nose repaired.

My husband was out of town so I had a lot of waiting to do by myself that day. After sitting for some time, I got out of my seat to stretch and walk down the hall. There by the entrance was an elderly lady standing with a paper in her hand looking very bewildered.

I knew that I had to ask her if she needed help. When I did, she cried and said that she wanted to pay her bill, but she couldn't find the financial office.

All of a sudden her whole story poured out as I walked her to the office. Her husband had died just two weeks before. When she walked into the hospital, the shock of being in the place where her husband had so recently died was overwhelming to her. My heart leaped with compassion for her as I put my arm around her to comfort her and help her through the trauma of that bill-paying excursion.

Jan had a choice to make when she glanced at the bewildered woman. She could have passed by on the other side; she could have looked the other way; she could have kept staring at her with curiosity, wondering what the woman would do next. Instead she noticed one who was hurting and in need. She felt compassion. She moved toward her. She listened. She gently did as much as a stranger could do to take care of this dear lady's "wound." She gave of herself, her time, and her love. She let the kindness and love of God minister healing through her to this dear wounded one.

Five biblical guidelines from Luke 10:25–37 for ministering to the needs of others are given in the following chart.

The Principle	The Samaritan	How It Applies to Me
1. Notice those around you who hurt.	Verses 30, 33: He saw him who had been left by robbers stripped, beaten, and half dead.	Train yourself to see beyond his or her obnoxious habits. See the circumstances, the hurts, the past rejections.

The Principle	The Samaritan	How It Applies to Me
2. Let your heart feel compassion.	Verse 33: He felt compassion.	Don't be afraid to put yourself in his or her position. Visualize the person as your mother or sister, father or brother.
3. Take time to consider their need.	Verse 34: He came to him.	Move toward the person, not away. Look and listen. Don't let obnoxious behavior make you pass by on the other side.
4. Take care of the wound.	Verse 34: He bandaged up his wounds, pouring oil and wine on them.	Wine for cleansing: Gently help him receive God's forgiveness for his past. Oil for healing: Let God minister grace through you (chapter 23). Bandage for protection: Give additional support while the wound heals.
5. Give continued affirmations of your care.	Verses 34, 35: From his own resources he gave his own beast, his own money, and his own time.	It will cost time, money, and personal inconvenience to reach out in love for others.

26

How to Show Love by Our Attitudes

How can we really love one another? One way of expressing it is by affirming the other person in his or her triad of personal-circle needs. A practical way of approaching this is to continually think how we can answer in a positive way the three questions the person is continually asking: (1) Does anyone love me? (2) Am I worth anything? (3) Can I do anything worthwhile? We communicate our answers to these questions by our attitudes. One of the most affirming attitudes I can have toward another is respect.

Respect by Appreciating Uniqueness

To respect a person is to appreciate his or her uniqueness as an individual. By listening and seeking to understand the person's viewpoint, I come to appreciate and accept as valid the individual's tastes, preferences, strengths, and even weaknesses. When I do this without criticism, without giving instant advice, and without quickly seeking to solve the problem, I communicate respect. And respect enhances self-worth. Paul Tournier points out, "All of us fear being judged or criticized, for no one is satisfied with himself."[12] Our sense of worth is fragile.

One wife wrote to me about how she realized her attitudes were affecting her husband's self-esteem and their marriage.

For twenty-five years of marriage, we had nothing but unhappiness, and yet I didn't know why. My husband and I had a poor relationship and virtually no communication. Every time I tried to converse with him he would storm off in anger after a few sentences and I would sit wondering, What did I do? What did I say? I was so unaware of my faults that I could never discern the reason for his actions.

Through the workshop I began to realize that maybe some of the fault lay with me, and not all with him. I began to pray as David did in the Psalms, "Lord, reveal to me my secret faults." Then my eyes began to open to the fact that I was damaging our relationship and his self-esteem by my attitudes. I would imply,

- *"I always think of it," making him feel incompetent.*
- *"I'm always right," which slammed shut his side of the conversation.*
- *"I already knew it," which made him feel inferior and stupid.*
- *"I have the best way," which lowered his self-esteem.*

Now that God has revealed these things to me, and I'm beginning to correct them, you wouldn't believe the change in the relationship and communication between us. We are even discussing spiritual matters and he was never interested in discussing them before.

Respect in an Atmosphere of Freedom

If we are to communicate respect—and thus love—to another, it has to be in an atmosphere of freedom. We must give the person space to grow.

This freedom is nurtured in the soil of unconditional acceptance. Or, in other words, my acceptance is not based on how he or she responds to me, how he meets (or doesn't meet) my needs, or if she does things my way. I give up my expectations of having the person respond in a certain way. I carry no "shoulds" and "oughts" in a bag marked "expectations." Having no expectations eliminates disappointment!

My mate, my children, even my friends, need to sense that I am releasing them to an appropriate level of independence. This level varies, especially with children. There is a certain right and proper independence at every age level that changes and increases as a child matures.

Others in my life must be released from any jealousy or possessiveness on my part. I must give them freedom to have other confidantes, to no longer need me, to walk to the beat of another drummer if this is what they choose. There may even come the time when parents have to release an adult child to marry someone they consider to be the wrong person or to practice a behavior they do not approve of.

A mother discovered a new level of independence that she needed to honor in her twelve-year-old daughter.

At the change of each season I go through my children's clothes and have them try on their things to see what fits, what they've outgrown, what they have, and what they need. It also provides a time for cleaning out and straightening drawers and closets.

Last spring when I came to my twelve-year-old daughter's clothes, I was in a big hurry to get that job done and go on to something else. She was uncooperative. After each piece was either tried on or held up, she'd lie down and I'd have to prod her on. I found that some clothes were still wearable, but she had not worn them. When I asked why, her only answer was, "I don't know."

I became upset and said, "It seems to me if I am willing to take my time, you at least ought to be willing to cooperate!" Finally, almost in tears, I left saying, "You can just do it yourself!"

If I had been more sensitive to her needs, I would have realized that, at twelve, she wanted just that—to do it herself. She felt she was old enough to make the decisions on her own. She was also modest and did not want to be dressing and undressing in front of me.

Fortunately I realized my mistake and her need immediately after my exit. So I went back, apologized, and told her I loved her and appreciated the fact that she wanted to take charge of her own things. She finished up in no time!

Respect through Sensitivity

Respect includes a sensitivity to the needs and rights of the other. For instance, we all need a certain amount of privacy and space, even the privilege of keeping legitimate secrets, as this girl explains.

A secret was one thing my mother never wanted me to have. She wanted to know everything. I saw how she treated the secrets of others. She would say, "I'm not supposed to share this, but . . ." So I knew I couldn't trust her.

One incident especially stands out in my memory. I had a diary as a teen and I expressed my thoughts quite freely in it. One day as I was reading it over, I found a note from Mother scolding me for what I had written and telling me what an ungrateful daughter I was.

I still can't believe she invaded my privacy like that and then even left a note to reprimand me. I was so angry when I found that note, that I stopped writing in the diary. I made the wall between us even thicker and kept her at a further distance. I needed privacy, and the more she pushed to get in, the more I pushed her away.

We must give others the privilege of including or excluding us as they will. We all have the capacity for only a limited number of intimate friends. The time and emotional energy we have very naturally limit our giving. Some people have a full circle of close friends and cannot add another. Give them the freedom to include or exclude you.

A daughter-in-law explained that since her mother-in-law had all boys, and since she was the first daughter-in-law, she had a wonderful relationship with her husband's mother. They spent much time together—shopping, visiting, and planning. "Now," she lamented, "things are so different. She doesn't seem interested in doing all those things together any more."

As we talked, I learned that in recent years several more daughters-in-law and a number of grandchildren had been added to the family. She came to see that it was not that the mother-in-law was disinterested, or that she had changed, but that her circumstances had changed. Now she needed to share her time with her other daughters-in-law and her grandchildren. These also have legitimately been added to her circle of time and friendships. Since her circle is only so big and since there are now many other close relatives, obviously she doesn't have the amount of time to give one person that she did previously.

When the daughter-in-law understood the full circle principle in regard to her mother-in-law, she realized it was not a personal rejection or disinterest, but a human impossibility to give the same amount of time to their friendship that she had previously. This understanding brought her great relief.

Respect Present Limitations

There is also a sense in which we need to respect the present limitations that put a boundary around the other person. It may be some inability, the lack of an essential skill, or a temporary struggle the person faces that drains his or her energies. Is his hearing impaired? Is her physical strength not on a par with yours?

Recognizing someone's limitations and struggles stimulates compassion and helps transform irritating situations into understanding and acceptance. Paul Tournier urges us to "Love . . . not so much for his qualities, as for his problems. . . . Understand what he missed in his childhood years and what he is still missing, and seek to fill that need."[13] That's all part of respect. And respect communicates love.

In addition to respect, a forgiving attitude is very essential for communicating love. Since we covered this so thoroughly in part 3, we'll not comment on it further here. You may want to review that section. The most important thing to remember is that respect and forgiveness are very important and basic attitudes in communicating love.

27

How to Show Love by Our Words

Words have a powerful effect on all three areas of our personal-circle needs. They can tear us down or build us up, be hurtful or helpful, positive or negative. By our careless remarks we can so easily cause any love that is in the other person's love cup to leak out and leave the cup bone dry.

Possibly one of the most powerful portions of Scripture that speaks to this is Ephesians 4:29, quoted from the NASB: "Let no unwholesome word proceed from your mouth, but only such a word as is good for edification according to the need of the moment, that it may give grace to those who hear." Words have a powerful effect on the hearer. Unwholesome words are hurtful and not good for edification. They do not meet the need of the moment, nor give grace to those who hear.

Hurtful Words

Let's take a look at some hurtful words that we may carelessly say to one another, words that undermine our sense of belonging.

- "You are always in my way!"
- "What are *you* doing here?"
- "If you do that once more, I'm going to . . ."

Negative words chip away at our healthy sense of self-worth.

- "Who do you think you are?"
- "Why did you leave the door open? What do you think this is, a barn?"
- "Are you always so shy?"
- "You are so absent-minded. You would forget your head if it weren't fastened on your shoulders."
- "No one will ever want to marry *you*."

Harmful words work quickly to destroy our sense of adequacy.

- "Can't you ever do anything right?"
- "How many times have I told you?"
- "Stupid! You're always breaking something."
- "You'll never learn. I'm wasting my breath on you."
- "The way you drive! How do you ever make it without me?"

Helpful Words

On the other hand, Proverbs 12:18 says, "Reckless words pierce like a sword, but the tongue of the wise brings healing" (NIV). So let's take a look at some positive words we can speak with a wise tongue, to bring healing to the wounds of another.

Wise words affirm our sense of belonging by giving us assurance that we are wanted, missed, loved, and appreciated.

- "It's not quite the same around here without you."
- "We sure missed you at church last week."
- "You have enriched my life."
- "You go sit down, Honey. I'll clean up."

A mother of four wrote,

My oldest girl told me that I gave more attention to the youngest girl than to the middle girl. There are many reasons for this, of course. She was the youngest and demanded more from me. The middle girl also seemed very independent. I have heard of the middle-child problem and I thanked my daughter for her insight and for sharing this with me.

Now I call my middle girl "Stuffin'." I explain to her that she is the good stuff in the sandwich. Now she knows when I call her Stuffin' she's the yummy-in-between!

Positive words give the other recognition as a worthwhile person.

- "That was so thoughtful of you to close the door behind you."
- "You were polite as you sat and listened without interruption."
- "I really appreciate you."
- "Thank you for your note. It brought me real joy."
- "What would you like to do? Where would you like to go?"

One wife told how a few words from her husband communicated a powerful message.

I dreaded going to the gynecologist. My husband and I talked about it and I asked him to pray that I would make the appointment and go. A few days later, in a kind, non-nagging way, he asked if I had an appointment yet. The day I was to go all he said was, "I love you." That said to me that he had been praying for me and he cared about how I was feeling.

A mother of six was feeling that she could never be of any use to the Lord because all she ever did was take care of her children.

I shared my feelings with my mother-in-law. She told me that if I could raise these six children to love the Lord and want to live for him, I would have done a missionary's job. This changed my attitude toward myself, my children, motherhood, and my home. I began to appreciate the important role of the mother, and it changed my whole sense of usefulness and purpose in life.

Another woman wrote,

One thing I have started to say in an encouraging, positive way is, "That's just like you!" For example, when my eight-year-old daughter deferred to a friend in a matter of turn-taking, allowing the friend the first turn, a chance came a few minutes later for me to take Ellen aside and say, "That was just like you, honey, to let Miriam have the first turn."

There are many occasions each day when I find I can positively affirm someone by saying, "That was just like you to . . ." Of course this could be misused, "That was just like you to forget to pick up your socks again." But obviously that's not the right idea!

A baby-sitter named Candy wrote me about some encouraging words she spoke to her young charge.

Four-year-old Randy was a big boy. He often heard, "My, isn't he big for his age!" or "Why are you always so clumsy?" One day when I was baby-sitting for him he accidentally knocked something over and grumbled, "Oh, I'm too big and clumsy!"

I quietly sat down to talk with him. "Randy, do you know about God?"

"Yes."

"Do you know that one day God said, 'And now let us have Randy. And when Randy is four years old he will be this high and this wide'?" Randy was listening with wide eyes. "How old are you, Randy?"

"Four."

"And how high are you and how wide?"

As this wonderful thought came through to him, Randy beamed with excitement. When his mother came home he met her at the door with, "And you know what, Mom? One day God said, 'And now let's have Randy, and when he's four years old he'll be this high and this wide.' And you know, Mom, I'm four years old and I'm this high and this wide!"

Randy thought, Oh, how good to know that I'm not too big. I'm not too clumsy. Randy was right on schedule with God's plans!

Confidence-Building Words

Healing words give us the confidence that we are performing according to our abilities.

- "Atta boy! That's great."
- "Good for you! You got home just in time."
- "You did a good job sweeping the deck."
- "It's not easy to do so much homework, but you are really sticking with it."

When Andy was complimented for his nice-looking jacket, his mother, who was standing nearby and heard it said, "Yes, he chose it himself. He picked out his own school clothes this year." Andy beamed, deeply appreciating that word of commendation and encouragement from his mother.

28

How to Show Love by Our Deeds

The family offers a beautiful opportunity to practice the principle of ministering to the needs of others. First there is the self-giving love that the partners have committed to one another. Then, when a child comes along, more opportunities arise for self-centeredness to give way to other-centeredness. Then, as more children arrive, more opportunities arise not only to be self-giving, ministering to the needs of more children, but also to train the little ones to be respectful and to minister to each other.

A grown woman tells how her father communicated his love by saving a small bag of useless treasures.

My parents divorced when I was nine and I was moved two thousand miles away—taking nothing with me. Four years later I was able to return to my father's home. My father was remarried and I was sure that I wouldn't mean the same to him now

*that he had more children. So upon arriving at their home I was
very fearful.*

*My father had a very special gift for my coming home that
washed away all my anxieties. While going through our be-
longings after the divorce, he came across my "treasures"—a
small bag that snapped closed that contained a broken ear-
ring, a few bobby pins, a car with no wheels, a plastic ring
that had long since lost its jewel at the top, and a fuzzy little
toy caterpillar.*

*When my father brought those treasures out for me, I knew
without a doubt that he loved me and wanted me. You see,
that's the only thing I had that linked me to my past. My father
had moved many times in that four-year period and could have
tossed what must have seemed like junk to most people, but
he loved his baby girl enough to keep it, in hopes of being able
to return it to me some day.*

*My father died only seven months after I was reunited with
him, but because of that gesture—a small bag of useless treasures—he will always live in my memories as a great and loving father. It feels so good to relive the memory.*

*I have two sons of my own now and their treasures will never
be junk to me. Hopefully one day their treasures will be memories for them too.*

A mother tells how she takes every chance she can to
show love to her teenage boys.

*My kitchen is a special place for love. When my big, teen-
age boys come snooping before dinner, looking in the pots
and saying, "What's cooking, Mom?" I make it an occasion to
give them a big hug or warm kiss. Even if my hands are full
of flour or I have many irons in the fire, I drop what I'm doing
and wash my hands. One son has come to expect this attention and often will even ask for a hug while I fix supper. We
have found that teenagers need to be hugged and kissed reg-*

ularly (not in front of friends, of course), even though they may not initiate it.

Another way to pour a little love into somebody else's love cup is to laugh at their jokes, even if they aren't very funny. Laugh as though they were funny because they intended them to be. Affirm their ability to be humorous.

I have enjoyed my husband's humor for the past eighteen years. I still consider him one of the funniest men alive. I truly enjoy his nuttiness and am usually the first one to laugh and °do it the loudest (if I'm not careful).

He informed me the other night that it really made him feel special to know I enjoyed his humor. He will joke with others that he married me because I laughed at his jokes, but there is some truth to that! He never goes too far with his joking, and has social sense about when to stop, so I can laugh with perfect assurance that he would never intentionally hurt or offend anyone.

Perhaps you'd like to devise a special love signal as this mother did.

I have devised a secret code with both of my two children to show and remind them that I love them. When we are in a crowded, public place or when I am busy with friends, we use our signal. My six-year-old boy and I share a wink; my ten-year-old girl and I share an "OK" sign. These are our secret messages for "I love you."

One day I pulled into the schoolyard and it happened to be recess. As I got out of the car, my little boy came running across the playground, smiling from ear to ear. He stopped at the edge of the playground just long enough to give me a big wink; then he ran back with his friends. What a neat feeling! This has become very special for me and the children.

Marilyn Pribus writes of the unique, homespun way their family has found to encourage ministering to each other instead of every member looking out for him- or herself.

My husband, Glenn, has a wonderful philosophy that we call "the theory of the love bucket." It is an easy concept for children to grasp, because it is something they can visualize. You see, everyone has a love bucket. If you are happy, and you have plenty of love to share, then your love bucket is brimming full. But when you are nervous or cross, gloomy or crotchety, it could be that yours is low.

The basic philosophy behind the love-bucket theory is simply this: Never let the sun set on an empty love bucket. It's not always easy, but it's always worth the effort.

When one of the boys is grouchy, it could be a cold coming on, but more likely it's a leaky love bucket. Dad's being away on a long trip, a bad spelling test, or not being invited to a birthday party can be especially hard on love buckets. Then it's time for a Danny day or a Nicky day. Everyone concentrates on filling Dan's or Nick's love bucket. Maybe one of his chores is done for him as a surprise. Perhaps he chooses the dinner menu. He might get to select the book for bedtime reading or make a call all his own to one of his grandmothers.

Usually the extra expression of love that has been there all along will chase away the grumbles. And it works! Reinforce undesirable behavior by rewarding it, you suggest? No, it really doesn't. In fact, far from encouraging selfishness, I've found that it makes the children more understanding and much more sensitive to the moods and feelings of others.

A serious loss such as moving away from good friends or a death in the family can knock the bottom right out of a love bucket so that it takes months to rebuild. When a child is confused or frightened by his or her feelings at such a time, it can be infinitely comforting to hear, "I'll help you mend your love bucket no matter how long it takes."

When a new baby gets too much attention, it can be reassuring to an older child to be told, "There's still plenty of love to keep your bucket full, don't you worry." If a child backs himself into a corner by being contrary and obstinate, you can work wonders if, instead of dueling verbally, you say, "I'll bet your love bucket isn't quite full today." (That even works with husbands.)

When our younger boy was only three, he understood exactly what I meant when I commented, "I think Daddy's love-bucket level is low." Or when I said, "Quit punching holes in your brother's love bucket." Or when I said, "My love bucket's so full, it's splashing all over."

I was really convinced, however, one day when I was not being so cheerful myself. In fact, I must admit I was being downright crabby. Dan was four at the time, and he came over to me, put his arms around my legs, looked up at me for a moment, then said earnestly to his brother, "I think it's time for a Mommy day."

Extra Grace for a Blended Family

As some of you well know, there are special situations that take extra grace and godly wisdom to know how to minister love. One stepmother wrote this to me:

What a blessing a wife and mother in a blended family can be if she is claiming personal-circle fullness in God himself. She can then lay down the battle of jealousy, hatred, immaturity, and insecurity that kills all relationships, and take up her divine assignment, realizing how God wants to use her influence in each life.

Once she can do this, especially in a blended marriage, then she can separate herself enough from the children and her husband and draw closer to God. I believe this is the key.

Then confusion in each member can be cleared up and, as each one finds his own worth in God's eyes, peace can enter this home.

It is very different trying to live the second time around, still carrying the old experiences somewhere in your heart and mind. It's not like a fresh new start. But God is especially able to do the impossible!

This wife and mother approaches the need to minister to her family with a special set of challenges. Rather than starting out the marriage with only one other to minister to, there may be many that are crying for your love. Also, any discord in a blended family is more complicated. The first wound remains open for a long time.

A child may feel responsibility or jealousy or guilt toward his natural parent. He may feel bitterness toward the stepparent and resent his or her authority. How important that this wife and mother in a blended family approaches her ministry daily with personal-circle fullness!

The Foundation: I Choose to Believe

How important for all of us, whatever our ministry, that we approach each day, each task, each circumstance, each relationship with personal-circle fullness and the mind-set to forgive our debtors. This is not only the broad basis for dealing with stress and letting us enjoy contentment and peace, but the only adequate foundation on which to build our ministry to others.

The God who promised, "My peace I give to you" (John 14:27), also said, "Do not merely look out for your own personal interests, but also for the interests of others" (Phil. 2:4 NASB).

Contentment and peace are not an end in themselves. They are the basis for fulfilling God's purpose for us in ministering to others in this stress-filled, needy world.

Enjoy his peace!

Minister his peace to others!

Now may the Lord of peace Himself continually grant you peace in every circumstance. The Lord be with you all!

2 Thessalonians 3:16 NASB

Study Guide

Chapters 1–2

Joseph

Read Genesis 37–50.

Expand Your Understanding

1. List some circumstances that could easily have triggered stress overload for Joseph.
2. Do you find any indication of resentment or bitterness in Joseph because of the many people who misused him?

Make Right Choices

1. What right choices did Joseph make?
2. What larger purpose of God could Joseph see (45:4–8)?
3. How did this help him in his response to his own stressful situations?

Jonah

Read
Jonah
1–4.

1. Why was Jonah running away from God (1:1–3; 3:10–4:2)?
2. List some things that happened over which Jonah had no control (1:4, 17; 2:10; 4:6–8).

1. What wrong choices did Jonah make (1:3; 4:1–11)?
2. What resulted in each case?
3. Try to express in your own words the handle for stress that Jonah found while he was in the great fish (Jonah 2).

*Your
Own
Life*

1. List any current circumstances in your life that, if managed improperly, could produce stress overload for you.
2. From your study of Joseph try to describe the handle for stress that God makes available to us as well.

1. Have you made any wrong choices in relation to your current circumstances?
2. Is there a choice you must make to go God's way in this situation?
3. Is there a need to deal with any resentment or bitterness?

Reach Out to Others

1. Be sensitive to the stressful circumstances of someone else today. Rather than quickly quoting a Bible verse to them, seek to understand and empathize with them.

I recently heard from a young woman,

When I lost my first baby through miscarriage two years ago, a Christian sister gave me a card with Romans 8:28 screaming out at me. I wasn't ready to accept that truth yet. Although I have since learned to rest in the comfort of all things working together for good, every time I see that verse my first reaction is hurt. It would have given me a greater comfort and started me on the road to acceptance if she had simply sat and mourned with me.

2. Ask God to help you see the events of other people's lives from their point of view. It may be a child rejected by a peer group; your husband who failed in a business venture; or a friend who was ignored, criticized, or misunderstood by another friend. Make yourself available to listen and care.

Chapters 3–5

Expand Your Understanding

1. Read Psalm 63. Where was David when he wrote this psalm (1 Sam. 23:15)? Using verses 1, 5, and 8 as key verses list three main points in the Psalm. From verses 2–4 how does his "thirsting" turn to "satisfaction"? What steps of choice and faith does he take in verses 5–8?

2. From the following verses write how one's desire is satisfied (Ps. 34:8–10; 37:4; John 4:13, 14; 6:32–35; 7:37–39).

3. Look up the following verses and write a statement (see chapter 3) as to how each one relates to personal-circle fullness (Ps. 84:11; Rom. 8:32; 2 Cor. 6:10; 2 Cor. 9:8; 1 Tim. 6:17).

Make Right Choices

1. Reread chapter 5. Write a prayer that declares to God that you are receiving his love for your need of belonging, his acceptance for your need of worth, and his power for your need of competence. Include some Scripture on which you will rest your faith.

2. What Scriptures come to mind to give you assurance that God and what he chooses to provide this moment are all you need for personal-circle fullness? Or, in your regular daily Bible reading notice any inference or reference to what we are calling personal-circle fullness. Write them down.

Reach Out to Others

1. Are you aware of someone who seems to have a deep, unfulfilled thirst or desire? Begin praying for him or her to become aware of the thirst and see God as the only one who can ultimately satisfy. You may want to use some of Paul's prayers: Ephesians 3:16–19; Colossians 1:9–12; 2 Thessalonians 3:5. Ask the Lord to give you a natural opportunity to share with him or her your own assurance of personal-circle fullness.

2. Find in the Psalms some of your favorite declarations of faith, such as, Psalm 23:1, Psalm 16:8, and Psalm 27:1. Ask the Lord to give you an opportu-

nity to share this concept of personal-circle fullness with someone else. Make it personal. Share
some of the concepts you wrote out in the "Make
Right Choices" section above and refer to some of
the Psalms you found to declare your faith.

Chapters 6–9

Expand Your Understanding

1. Read the following portions of Scripture about
   Abraham and answer the questions (Gen. 15:1–6;
   17:15–17; 18:10–14; 22:18; Rom. 4:3, 18–22). What
   were Abraham's impossible circumstances? What
   did Abraham choose to believe? Which verses state
   this? What was God's part in resolving this difficult situation? What did he expect of Abraham?
2. From chapter 9, list the stabilizing truths about
   God on which we can rest our faith. Use this list as
   your declaration of faith each morning this week.

Make Right Choices

1. Is there a thorn in your life that makes you feel
   inadequate and weak (see chapter 6 and 2 Cor.
   12:7–10)? Are you willing to choose God's all-sufficient grace as Paul did, even if the thorn remains?
   Personalize Paul's declaration of faith and his
   choice by writing in your own personal weakness
   or problem.
       "Therefore most gladly I will rather boast in my
   ———, that the power of Christ may rest upon me.
   Therefore, I take pleasure in———, for Christ's
   sake" (2 Cor. 12:9–10).
2. Is there a difficult situation you are finding hard
   to cope with right now? Try to state it in a brief
   sentence. Below that sentence write your specific

declaration of personal-circle fullness as it relates to this situation: "I choose to believe————."
Now note the specific things the Lord has provided already regarding this situation.

3. Write out an instance from your life (past or present) where you were able to choose personal-circle fullness. What were the results in you, in the other person, and in the circumstance? Or write about a time you reached out to try to satisfy your deep longings with something God was not providing at that moment. Did it satisfy?

Reach Out to Others

1. To increase your discernment in balancing this truth and to enable you to better reach out in helping others, read the story at the beginning of chapter 7 and answer the following questions. Was it right and important for the woman to declare her own personal-circle fullness as she met the situation? What did this do for her own attitude and spirit? Does she have any responsibility for action in relation to her husband?

2. Study figure 8.2 in chapter 8. Which side of this truth do you see as your weak spot? Decide on one thing you can do to increase your strength in that area. For example: You have few friends but you have been able to find contentment and companionship in your relationship with Jesus Christ. To balance that, reach out this week to make some small contact with a potential friend.

Chapters 10–13

Expand Your Understanding

1. Read Nehemiah 1:3; 2:4–5, 17–20; 4:1–23. What did Nehemiah believe God was calling him to do?

Who began putting negative input into the belief system of Nehemiah and his workers? What was some of that negative input? What positive input did Nehemiah give to fuel their faith (Neh. 2:18, 20; 4:14, 20)?

2. King Solomon is a classic example of one who did a lot of cistern digging, only to find in the end that they were all broken. From Ecclesiastes 1:16–18; 2:1–11; and 5:10–11 list the cisterns Solomon reached out to for satisfaction, peace, and contentment. What was his conclusion?

   Many commentators agree that Ecclesiastes 5:18–20 expresses the godly attitude toward life: approaching life from a position of personal-circle fullness in Christ rather than digging cisterns. With this in mind list the things God has chosen to provide in these verses.

3. Read these two accounts that show how Satan affects our belief system: 1 Chronicles 21:1–17 and Acts 5:1–11. In each case, what did Satan do? What were the results for the people?

   What are we to do when Satan tempts us (James 4:7)? How can we do this (Eph. 6:10–20)? List each piece of this armor with a comment on what each means. What are we to add to the armor (vv. 18–19)?

4. What means does the world around us use to "squeeze us into its own mold"? How can we avoid this and counteract its influence?

Make Right Choices

1. Read Psalm 55. What was David's "If only, . . ." (v. 6)? Was his "if only" a likely possibility? What was he trying to escape? How did he begin to think more clearly (vv. 16–21)?

His final "statement of trust" is in verses 22 and 23. Write this in your own words.

2. Think through the events and involvements of your life at the present time. Write down any "if-onlys" that you are perhaps unconsciously holding on to, believing they would be an escape from unwanted circumstances. Now write a statement expressing your trust in the Lord and in his ability to handle the problem.

Reach Out to Others

1. To become aware of how we are inputting the belief system of others, choose one person in a close relationship to you. Write down specific ways you are responding to the three basic questions he or she needs answered from you. Do you love me? Do you care, understand, and feel for me? Can I do anything worthwhile?

2. What improvement do you need to make in your response to this person? Write out specific actions you will take in each of the three areas to communicate love, acceptance, and confidence in him or her.

Chapters 14–16

Expand Your Understanding

1. Read Luke 12:13–21. How does this parable illustrate our "endless search for something more"?

2. In verses 16–19 what words or phrases show that the man had an abundance of earthly goods? Who did he speak to in verse 19? Was he giving his soul the kind of food that would satisfy its deep longings?

3. What were some of the broken cisterns he dug? Find a phrase in verse 21 that expresses personal-circle fullness in different words.
4. Describe the false security that the rich man of the Luke 12 parable tried to convince himself of through his "self-talk" (vv. 17–19). In contrast, what was God's truth (vv. 20–21)?
5. What could he have asked himself to judge whether his beliefs were right or wrong (see chapter 14)?

Make Right Choices

1. Read Luke 12:22–34. What are some of the things that God has chosen to provide for us as mentioned in these verses? What are we to go after (v. 31)? What does that mean to you?
2. What have you been saying to yourself about your own person, about God, or about the past or current circumstances of your life? Write down several recent conversations you've had with yourself.
3. Make a judgment: Does what I'm thinking harmonize with God's thinking or is it Satan's lie?
4. Write a statement of God's truth about the situation. Devise a method of recalling this in times of temptation and doubt.

Reach Out to Others

1. Ask a trusted friend to help you hear what you're saying to yourself. Let him or her help you judge your belief about the situation and be a support to you as you seek to let God's truth take over.
2. Evaluate what you think God may be teaching you through your present circumstances. How do you see this relating to someone else in your circle of family or friends? Pray for and plan an opportunity to reach out to help another.

Chapters 17–19

Expand Your Understanding

Read 2 Samuel 11 and 12 and consider the following:
1. In chapter 11 we see how one sin led to another in David's life. Briefly list these sins (see also 12:9–10).
2. David needed to become aware of his sin. How did God use Nathan in this (12:1–7)? How did David feel about the rich man's actions toward the poor man?
3. To whom was the rich man debtor? To whom was David debtor (12:7–8)?
4. How did the Lord respond when David acknowledged his sin (12:13–25)?

Make Right Choices

1. List David's choices in the following verses in chapters 11 and 12 of 2 Samuel under either the right choices column or the wrong choices column.

	Right Choices	*Wrong Choices*
11:3		
11:4		
11:15		
11:27		
12:13		
12:16		
12:20		
12:22		

2. Read Psalm 51 to see how David felt about his sin. What right choice did David make concerning his sin in Psalm 32:3–5? How did God respond?

3. Do you need to receive God's full forgiveness through Christ? Read again the three verses and consider the prayer at the beginning of chapter 18.

Reach Out to Others

1. Plan two definite ways you can pay your debt of love to one specific person. See some elements of love listed in chapter 18.
2. Read again chapter 19 asking the Lord to zero in on some relationship in which you feel the love that is due you has not been paid. Try to write two or three sentences expressing how you feel about this debtor. Are you ready to choose to forgive and cancel the debt?

Chapters 20–22

Expand Your Understanding

1. What did the Israelites feel God owed them in the wilderness (Exod. 15:22–24; 16:2–3; and Num. 21:4–5)? Was God debtor to them? Explain.
2. In Psalm 73 Asaph expressed what he saw as inequity: The prosperity of the wicked while the righteous are "stricken" and "chastened" (v. 14). What does he imply God owed him (vv. 1–14)?
3. What attitude had taken over (v. 21) because he was holding God debtor to him?
4. What were his conclusions (vv. 16–28) after he had mulled it over and began to see things from God's perspective?

Make Right Choices

1. Is there any way you are holding God as your debtor right now? Is there a long-prayed prayer

that he should have answered by now? A person he has allowed in your life who causes you untold agony and distress? Would you choose now to let God be God in your life? To release God from the debt, to no longer expect him to pay what you have come to believe he owes you?

2. Is there a past failure or sin that continues to haunt you and keep you from experiencing contentment and peace? In one brief sentence, state it to yourself and to God. Take the steps outlined in chapter 22.

Reach Out to Others

1. Do you know someone who has been hurt deeply and has obviously responded in resentment and bitterness to the Lord and to the other person? Will you commit yourself to pray for and show acts of love to that hurting one?

2. Write a statement or a prayer in response to each of the items suggested under "Put Forgiveness into Action" in chapter 21. If you have a specific person or situation in mind, zero in on that in your responses. Take any steps necessary and appropriate to correct this with the person you wronged.

Chapters 23–25

Expand Your Understanding

1. Read the following Scripture verses and answer the following questions. Name the person. Describe how he or she was either a negative or positive example of the misbelief that I must watch out for Number One. Were any results obvious?

> Genesis 13:8–18
> Ecclesiastes 1:1; 2:10–11

Matthew 1:18–21
Matthew 19:16–22
Acts 20:24
2 Corinthians 8:9
Philippians 2:19–22
Philippians 3:7–8

2. In contrast to this misbelief, Jesus describes true belief in Matthew 16:24–26. Read this and write a paraphrase in words that a child could understand.

Make Right Choices

From the verses below, describe situations where God is asking us to choose to put the other person first, instead of ourselves. If we choose to put the other person's needs above our own, what action will we take in the situation?

1. Romans 15:1; 1 Corinthians 9:22
   When the other person is . . .
   My action should be . . .
2. Galatians 6:2
   When the other person is . . .
   My action should be . . .
3. James 2:15–16; 1 John 3:17
   When the other person needs . . .
   My action should be . . .
4. Luke 17:3–4
   When the other person needs . . .
   My action should be . . .

Reach Out to Others

1. List the four categories of need you discovered under the "Make Right Choices" section above.

2. Next to each write the name of a person (or group) in your circle of acquaintance and/or influence who may have that need.

3. Write a sentence by each name indicating how you will respond to each one's needs.

Chapters 26–28

Expand Your Understanding

1. Look up these verses and make three lists: *Attitudes of Love*, *Words of Love*, and *Deeds of Love* List the specific attitude or the type of word or deed of love described in the following verses.

Ruth 2:11	Proverbs 17:9
Isaiah 44:22	Matthew 10:42
Luke 4:22	John 6:5–11
John 13:3–5	John 15:9–11
Acts 9:36	Acts 11:23
Acts 16:33–34	Romans 12:15
Ephesians 4:2, 32	Colossians 3:12–13
James 1:27	

2. What are some ways that words can hurt and be harmful? Look up these verses in several Bible versions and describe what you think each means.
   Job 19:2
   Psalm 36:3
   Acts 15:24

Make Right Choices

1. List the qualities of love expressed positively and negatively in 1 Corinthians 13:4–7 and make two lists: *Love Is (or Does)* and *Love Is Not (or Does Not)*.

2. Consider a person you sometimes find it hard to love. Pray through the two lists, asking God to show you where your love falls short. Ask him to work in you this kind of love.

Reach Out to Others

1. Read Philippians 1:9. What two things does this verse say our love should be growing (abounding) in? How can you apply this to your love for spouse, child, friend, and so forth?
2. From these verses discover what is to be our respectful response to specific limitations, handicaps, or problems we see in others. List the need and what our response should be.

    Job 4:3–4
    Isaiah 35:3–4
    Galatians 6:1
    1 Thessalonians 5:14
    Hebrews 12:12–13

NOTES

1. Lawrence Crabb, *Basic Principles of Biblical Counseling* (Grand Rapids: Zondervan Publishing House, 1975), 66–67.

2. From *Our Daily Bread,* July 5, 1981 (Grand Rapids: Radio Bible Class, 1981).

3. J. Sidlow Baxter, *His Part and Ours* (Grand Rapids: Zondervan Publishing House, 1959), 131.

4. J. Sidlow Baxter, *Awake My Heart* (Grand Rapids: Zondervan Publishing House, 1959), 244.

5. From the hymn, "I Heard the Voice of Jesus Say," by Horatius Bonar, *Hymns for the Living Church* (Carol Stream, Ill.: Hope Publishing Co., 1974), 309.

6. Haddon W. Robinson, *Psalm Twenty-three* (Chicago: Moody Press, 1968), 51.

7. F. B. Meyer, *Great Verses through the Bible* (Grand Rapids: Zondervan Publishing House, 1960), 97.

8. V. Raymond Edman, *They Found the Secret* (Grand Rapids: Zondervan Publishing House, 1960), 97.

9. From the hymn, "Abide with Me," by Henry F. Lyte, *Worship and Service Hymnal* (Chicago: Hope Publishing Co., 1957), 148.

10. From the hymn, "At the Cross," by Isaac Watts, *Worship and Service Hymnal* (Chicago: Hope Publishing Co., 1957), 66.

11. John Henry Jowett, *My Daily Meditation* (LaVerne, Calif.: El Camino Press for First Church of the Nazarene, Pasadena, Calif.), 117.

12. Paul Tournier, *To Understand Each Other* (Richmond, Va.: John Knox Press, 1967), 22.

13. Ibid., 33.

For more information on seminars taught by Verna Birkey, write

Enriched Living
P.O. Box 3039
Kent, WA 98032